Microsoft WINDOWS 8

INTRODUCTORY

Microsoft® WINDOWS 8

INTRODUCTORY

Steven M. Freund
Raymond E. Enger
Corinne L. Hoisington

COURSE TECHNOLOGY
CENGAGE Learning®

SHELLY CASHMAN SERIES®

Australia • Brazil • Japan • Korea • Mexico • Singapore • Spain • United Kingdom • United States

COURSE TECHNOLOGY
CENGAGE Learning

Microsoft© Windows® 8 Introductory
Steven M. Freund
Raymond E. Enger
Corinne L. Hoisington

Editor-in-Chief: Marie Lee
Executive Editor: Kathleen McMahon
Senior Product Manager: Emma Newsom
Associate Product Manager: Crystal Parenteau
Editorial Assistant: Sarah Ryan
Print Buyer: Julio Esperas
Director of Production: Patty Stephen
Content Project Manager: Jennifer Feltri-George
Development Editor: Lyn Markowicz
Senior Brand Manager: Elinor Gregory
Market Development Manager: Kristie Clark
Market Development Manager: Gretchen Swann
Marketing Coordinator: Amy McGregor
QA Manuscript Reviewers: John Freitas, Serge Palladino
Art Director: GEX Publishing Services, Inc.
Cover Designer: Lisa Kuhn, Curio Press, LLC
Cover Photo: Tom Kates Photography
Compositor: Jenna Gray, PreMediaGlobal
Copyeditor: Karen Annett
Proofreader: Andrea Schein
Indexer: Alexandra Nickerson

© 2014 Course Technology, Cengage Learning

ALL RIGHTS RESERVED. No part of this work covered by the copyright herein may be reproduced, transmitted, stored or used in any form or by any means graphic, electronic, or mechanical, including but not limited to photocopying, recording, scanning, digitizing, taping, Web distribution, information networks, or information storage and retrieval systems, except as permitted under Section 107 or 108 of the 1976 United States Copyright Act, without the prior written permission of the publisher.

> For product information and technology assistance, contact us at
> **Cengage Learning Customer & Sales Support, 1-800-354-9706**
> For permission to use material from this text or product, submit all requests online at **cengage.com/permissions**
> Further permissions questions can be emailed to **permissionrequest@cengage.com**

Library of Congress Control Number: 2012953439

ISBN-13: 978-1-285-16313-0

ISBN-10: 1-285-16313-3

Course Technology
20 Channel Center Street
Boston, MA 02210
USA

Cengage Learning is a leading provider of customized learning solutions with office locations around the globe, including Singapore, the United Kingdom, Australia, Mexico, Brazil, and Japan. Locate your local office at: **international.cengage.com/region**

Cengage Learning products are represented in Canada by Nelson Education, Ltd.

Visit our website **www.cengage.com/ct/shellycashman** to share and gain ideas on our textbooks!

To learn more about Course Technology, visit **www.cengage.com/coursetechnology**

Purchase any of our products at your local college store or at our preferred online store **www.cengagebrain.com**

Printed in the United States of America
1 2 3 4 5 6 18 17 16 15 14 13

Microsoft® WINDOWS 8
INTRODUCTORY

Contents

Preface   vii

MICROSOFT WINDOWS 8

CHAPTER ONE
Getting Started with Windows 8

Objectives	WIN 1
What is Windows 8?	WIN 2
Overview	WIN 3
Multiple Editions of Windows 8	WIN 3
Navigating Using Touch or a Mouse	WIN 4
Using a Touch Screen	WIN 4
Using an On-Screen Keyboard	WIN 5
Using a Mouse	WIN 6
Scrolling	WIN 6
Using Keyboard Shortcuts	WIN 7
Starting Windows 8	WIN 7
To Sign In to an Account	WIN 8
Exploring the Start Screen	WIN 10
Working with Apps	WIN 11
To Run an App Using the Start Screen	WIN 11
To Navigate within an App	WIN 12
Using Charms	WIN 15
To Return to the Start Screen	WIN 15
Working with Apps	WIN 16
To Switch between Apps	WIN 16
Understanding How to Exit Apps	WIN 17
To Display the Windows Desktop	WIN 17
The Windows 8 Desktop	WIN 18
To Run the File Explorer	WIN 19
To Return to the Start Screen	WIN 19
To Move a Tile	WIN 20
To Resize a Tile	WIN 21
To Run an App Using the Search Box	WIN 23
To Search the Internet Using a Charm	WIN 25
To Search an App Using a Charm	WIN 28
Share Using a Charm	WIN 30
To View Sharing Options Using a Charm	WIN 30
Free and Paid Apps	WIN 31
To Install an App	WIN 31
Using Windows Help and Support	WIN 33
To Start Windows Help and Support	WIN 33
To Browse Help	WIN 36
Shutting Down Windows	WIN 37
To Sign Out of an Account	WIN 37
To Shut Down the Computer	WIN 39
Chapter Summary	WIN 40
Apply Your Knowledge	WIN 41
Extend Your Knowledge	WIN 42
In the Lab	WIN 43
Cases and Places	WIN 47

CHAPTER TWO
Windows 8 File and Folder Management

Objectives	WIN 49
Introduction	WIN 50
Overview	WIN 50
The Computer Folder Window	WIN 50
To Open and Maximize the Computer Folder Window	WIN 51
To Display Properties for the Local Disk (C:) Drive in the Details Pane	WIN 52
To Display the Local Disk (C:) Properties Dialog Box	WIN 53
To Close the Local Disk (C:) Properties Dialog Box	WIN 54
To Switch Folders Using the Address Bar	WIN 55
To View the Contents of a Drive	WIN 56
To Preview the Properties of a Folder	WIN 57
To Display Properties for the Windows Folder in the Details Pane	WIN 57
To Display All of the Properties of the Windows Folder	WIN 58
To View the Contents of a Folder	WIN 59
Searching for Files and Folders	WIN 59
To Search for a File and Folder in a Folder Window	WIN 60
To Clear the Search Box	WIN 61
To Use Shake to Minimize and Restore All Windows	WIN 62
To Use Snap to Maximize Windows	WIN 63
To Restore a Window	WIN 64

v

The Pictures Library	WIN 65
Item Check Boxes	WIN 66
To Search for Pictures	WIN 66
To Copy Files to the Pictures Library	WIN 67
To Create a Folder in the Pictures Library	WIN 69
To Move Multiple Files into a Folder	WIN 71
To Refresh the Image on a Folder	WIN 72
To View and Change the Properties of a Picture	WIN 72
To View a Picture in the Photos App	WIN 75
To View Your Pictures as a Slide Show	WIN 76
To End a Slide Show	WIN 77
Zipping Files and Folders	WIN 78
To Zip a Folder	WIN 78
To View the Contents of a Zipped Folder	WIN 79
Chapter Summary	WIN 80
Apply Your Knowledge	WIN 81
Extend Your Knowledge	WIN 82
In the Lab	WIN 84
Cases and Places	WIN 88

CHAPTER THREE
Personalizing Windows

Objectives	WIN 89
Introduction	WIN 90
Overview	WIN 90
User Account	WIN 90
What Is a Local Account?	WIN 91
What Is a Microsoft Account?	WIN 91
To Create a Microsoft Account	WIN 92
What Is Cloud Computing?	WIN 94
Setting up User Accounts	WIN 94
To Add a Local Account	WIN 94
To Add a Microsoft Account	WIN 98
Personalizing the Lock and Start Screens	WIN 100
To Personalize the Lock Screen	WIN 100
To Change the Start Screen Color Scheme	WIN 102
To Change the Start Screen Background Pattern	WIN 103
Adding a Picture Password	WIN 104
To Create a Picture Password	WIN 104
Is a Picture Password Secure?	WIN 108
Customizing the Start Screen	WIN 108
To Display All Apps	WIN 109
To Run an App from the Apps List	WIN 110
To Pin an App to the Start Screen	WIN 110
To Unpin an App from the Start Screen	WIN 113
To Turn Off a Live Tile	WIN 114
Managing Tile Layout	WIN 115
To Zoom to View Tile Groups	WIN 115
To Create a New Tile Group	WIN 117
To Move a Tile to a Different Tile Group	WIN 118
To Reorder Tile Groups	WIN 118
To Name a Tile Group	WIN 119
To Sign Out of an Account and Shut Down the Computer	WIN 122
Chapter Summary	WIN 122
Apply Your Knowledge	WIN 123
Extend Your Knowledge	WIN 124
In the Lab	WIN 125
Cases and Places	WIN 128

Appendix

APPENDIX A
Creating a Microsoft Account

Introduction	APP 1
To Create a Microsoft Account	APP 1

APPENDIX B
Windows 8 Security

Introduction	APP 9
To Display the Windows Action Center	APP 9
Understanding the Action Center	APP 13
Managing Windows Firewall	APP 13
To Open the Windows Firewall Window	APP 14
To Allow a Feature through the Firewall	APP 14
To Disallow a Feature through the Firewall	APP 17
Windows Update	APP 19
To Install Updates Automatically	APP 19
Protecting against Computer Viruses and Malware	APP 21
To Scan Using Windows Defender	APP 21
To View the Windows Defender Settings for Automatic Scanning	APP 24
Summary	APP 24
Index	IND 1

Preface

The Shelly Cashman Series® offers the finest textbooks in computer education. We are proud of the fact that our Microsoft Windows 3.1, Microsoft Windows 95, Microsoft Windows 98, Microsoft Windows 2000, Microsoft Windows XP, and Microsoft Windows Vista and Windows 7 books have been so well received by students and instructors. With each new edition of our Windows books, we have made significant improvements based on the software and comments made by instructors and students.

Windows 8 introduces a brand new way of interacting with computers and mobile devices such as tablets and smart phones. The new Windows 8 interface, which includes tiles, charms, and apps, will completely revolutionize how people work. This Windows 8 text not only teaches this new interface and approach in a way that is easiest for students to learn, but it also incorporates many important concepts such as file management and

Objectives of This Textbook

Microsoft® Windows® 8: Introductory is intended for a first course that offers an introduction to Windows 8. No experience with a computer is assumed, and no mathematics beyond the high school freshman level is required.

The objectives of this book are:

- To offer a comprehensive presentation of Microsoft Windows 8
- To expose students to practical examples of the computer as a useful tool
- To acquaint students with the proper procedures to manage and organize document storage options for coursework, professional purposes, and personal use
- To help students discover the underlying functionality and customization options of Windows 8 so that they can become more productive
- To develop an exercise-oriented approach that allows learning by doing

critical thinking in greater detail. Recognizing that the new features and functionality of Microsoft Windows 8 would impact the way that students are taught skills, the Shelly Cashman Series development team carefully reviewed our pedagogy and analyzed its effectiveness in teaching today's student. An extensive customer survey produced results confirming what the series is best known for: its step-by-step, screen-by-screen instructions, its project-oriented approach, and the quality of its content.

We learned, though, that students entering computer courses today are different than students taking these classes just a few years ago. Students today read less, but need to retain more. They need not only to be able to perform skills, but to retain those skills and know how to apply them to different settings. Today's students need to be continually engaged and challenged to retain what they're learning.

As a result, we've renewed our commitment to focusing on the user and how they learn best. This commitment is reflected in every change we've made to our Windows 8 books.

Distinguishing Features

A Proven Pedagogy with an Emphasis on Project Planning
The project orientation is strengthened by the use of Plan Ahead boxes that encourage critical thinking about how to proceed at the beginning of each chapter. Step-by-step instructions with supporting screens guide students through the steps. Instructional steps are supported by the Q&A, Experiment Step, and BTW features.

A Visually Engaging Book that Maintains Student Interest
The step-by-step tasks, with supporting figures, provide a rich visual experience for the student. Call-outs on the screens that present both explanatory and navigational information provide students with information they need when they need to know it.

Supporting Reference Materials (Appendices)
The appendices provide additional information about Windows 8, such as the security features and networking.

Integration of the World Wide Web
The World Wide Web is integrated into the Windows 8 learning experience through step-by-step instruction on Internet Explorer, as well as the several additional features.

End-of-Chapter Student Activities
Extensive end of chapter activities provide a variety of reinforcement opportunities for students where they can apply and expand their skills through individual and group work.

Instructor Resources

The Instructor Resources include both teaching and testing aids. These resources are posted to the instructor's resource page found on www.cengage.com

Instructor's Manual Includes lecture notes summarizing the chapter sections, figures and boxed elements found in every chapter, teacher tips, classroom activities, lab activities, and quick quizzes in Microsoft Word files.

Syllabus Easily customizable sample syllabi that cover policies, assignments, exams, and other course information.

Figure Files Illustrations for every figure in the textbook in electronic form.

Powerpoint Presentations A multimedia lecture presentation system that provides slides for each chapter. Presentations are based on chapter objectives.

Solutions to Exercises Includes solutions for all end-of-chapter and chapter reinforcement exercises.

Test Bank Test Banks include 112 questions for every chapter, featuring objective-based and critical thinking question types, and including page number references and figure references, when appropriate.

Data Files for Students Includes all the files that are required by students to complete the exercises.

Additional Activities for Students Consists of Chapter Reinforcement Exercises, which are true/false, multiple-choice, and short answer questions that help students gain confidence in the material learned.

CourseNotes
Course Technology's CourseNotes are six-panel quick reference cards that reinforce the most important concepts and features of a software application in a visual and user-friendly format. CourseNotes serve as a great reference tool during and after the student completes the course. CourseNotes are available for software applications, such as Adobe, Microsoft Office, and Windows 8. There are also topic-based CourseNotes available for Best Practices in Social Networking, Hot Topics in Technology, and Web 2.0. Visit www.cengage.com/ct/coursenotes to learn more!

SAM: Skills Assessment Manager
SAM is designed to help bring students from the classroom to the real world. It allows students to train and test on important computer skills in an active, hands-on environment.

SAM's easy-to-use system includes powerful interactive exams, training and projects on the most commonly used Microsoft® Office applications. SAM simulates the Office 2013 application environment, allowing students to demonstrate their knowledge and think through the skills by performing real-world tasks such as bolding word text or setting up slide transitions. Add in live-in-the-application projects and students are on their way to truly learning and applying skills to business-centric document.

Designed to be used with the Shelly Cashman Series, SAM includes handy page references, so students can print helpful study guides that match the Shelly Cashman Series textbooks used in class. For instructors, SAM also includes robust scheduling and reporting features.

Textbook Walk-Through

Step-by-step instructions now provide a context beyond the point-and-click. Each step provides information on why students are performing each task, or what will occur as a result.

Starting Windows 8 **WIN** 9

Windows Chapter 1

1
- Tap, slide, or click the lock screen (Figure 1–5) to display a sign-in screen.

lock screen

11:05
Monday, October 1

Figure 1–5

2
- Tap or click the user icon (for SC Series, in this case) on the sign-in screen, which depending on settings, either will display a second sign-in screen that contains a password text box (Figure 1–6) or will display the Windows Start screen.

Q&A
Why do I not see a user icon?
Your computer may require you to type a user name instead of tapping or clicking an icon.

What is a text box?
A text box is a rectangular box in which you type text.

Why does my screen not show a password text box?
Your account does not require a password.

sign-in screen

selected user account

SC Series

user account icon

Password

Submit button

password text box

Figure 1–6

Explanatory callouts summarize what is happening on screen.

Navigational callouts in red show students where to click.

Q&A boxes offer questions students may have when working through the steps and provide additional information about what they are doing right where they need it.

WIN 10 **Windows Chapter 1** Getting Started with Windows 8

3
- If Windows 8 displays a password text box, type your password in the text box and then tap or click the Submit button to sign in your account and display the Windows 8 Start screen (Figure 1–7).

Q&A

Why does my Start screen look different from the one shown in Figure 1–7?
The Windows 8 Start screen is customizable, and your school or employer may have modified the screen to meet its needs. Also, your screen resolution, which affects the size of the elements on the screen, may differ from the screen resolution used in this book. Later in this chapter, you will learn how to change screen resolution.

How do I type if my tablet has no keyboard?
You can use your fingers to press keys on a keyboard that appears on the screen, called an on-screen keyboard, or you can purchase a separate physical keyboard that attaches to or wirelessly communicates with the tablet.

Figure 1–7

Exploring the Start Screen

The Windows 8 Start screen provides a scrollable space for you to access apps that have been pinned to the Start screen (shown in Figure 1–7). Pinned apps appear as tiles on the Start screen. In addition to running apps, you can perform tasks such as pinning apps (placing tiles) on the Start screen, moving the tiles around the Start screen, and unpinning apps (removing tiles) from the Start screen.

A tile is shown as a rectangle or square on the Start screen. Tapping or clicking a tile will run the app associated with the tile. **Live tiles** are tiles that when configured, update the tile with information while the Start screen is displayed. For example, if you configure the Weather app to your location, the tile will update with current weather conditions in your city.

Textbook Walk-Through

Other Ways boxes that follow many of the step sequences explain the other ways to complete the task presented.

Extend Your Knowledge projects at the end of each chapter allow students to extend and expand on the skills learned within the chapter. Students use critical thinking to experiment with new skills to complete each project.

WIN 12 Windows Chapter 1 Getting Started with Windows 8

2
- Tap or click the Allow button to allow the Weather app to use the current location (Figure 1–9).
- If your location cannot be detected, type your current city in the Enter Location text box, and then click your city in the drop-down list that appears.

current weather information

background varies based on current location

Figure 1–9

Other Ways
1. Tap or click Search charm on Charms bar, type app name in Search box, tap or click app name in results list

To Navigate within an App

To navigate within an app, you can use gestures or the scroll bar to see more of the app, or you can display the Navigation bar for an app. In the Weather app, the Navigation bar lets you move from the Home screen to other places, and even displays world weather. *Why? You may intend to travel or you may be interested in seeing the weather in a different location.*

The following steps display the current world weather information.

WIN 42 Windows Chapter 3 Getting Started with Windows 8

Extend Your Knowledge

Extend the skills you learned in this chapter and experiment with new skills. You will use Help to complete the assignment.

Using Help

Instructions: Use Windows Help and Support to perform the following tasks.
1. Find Help about Windows shortcuts by typing `shortcuts` in the Search text box and then clicking the Search button (Figure 1–58). Tap or click the result titled 'Copy or move files and folders' and then answer the following questions:
   a. What keyboard shortcut is used to copy a file?
   b. What keyboard shortcut is used to paste a file?
   c. How do you display a shortcut menu?

Chapter Summary WIN 43

2. Use Windows Help and Support to answer the following questions:
   a. What is Windows Defender?
   b. What is Windows Firewall?
   c. What settings can you control in Family Safety?
   d. What are five ways to protect your computer from viruses and other threats?
   e. What is a user account?
   f. What is the difference between a local account and a Microsoft account?
3. Use the Search text box in Windows Help and Support to answer the following questions:
   a. How do you turn on Windows Firewall?
   b. How do you pin a program to the taskbar?
   c. How do you set up a home network in Windows?
   d. How do you add a printer?
4. The tools to solve a problem while using Windows 8 are called troubleshooters. Use Windows Help and Support to find information about troubleshooters, and answer the following questions:
   a. What problems does the Printer troubleshooter allow you to resolve?
   b. List two additional Windows 8 troubleshooters.
5. Close the Windows Help and Support window.

> The in-depth **In the Lab** assignments require students to utilize the chapter concepts and techniques to solve problems.

In the Lab

Use the guidelines, concepts, and skills presented in this chapter to increase your knowledge of Windows 8. Labs are listed in order of increasing difficulty.

Lab 1: Using Windows Help and Support
Problem: You have a few questions about using Windows and would like to answer these questions

Chapter Summary WIN 47

Cases and Places

Apply your creative thinking and problem-solving skills to design and implement a solution.

1: Assessing Windows 8 Compatibility
Academic
You work part-time as a lab technician in your school's computer lab. Your boss wants to upgrade several computers in the lab and has asked you to investigate. You know that the Windows 8 operating system can be installed only on computers found in the Windows 8 Hardware Compatibility List. Locate three older personal computers. Look for them in your school's computer lab, at a local business, or in your house. Use the Windows website on the Internet to locate the Windows 8 Compatibility Center. Check each computer against the list and write a brief report summarizing your results.

2: Sharing Your Pictures
Personal
You recently attended your high school reunion, and your friend has asked for your help. She wants to send photos to several classmates via email messages, and is not sure how best to proceed. Using Windows Help and Support and the keywords, digital pictures, locate the "How to use Windows Photo Viewer" article. In a brief report, summarize the steps required to send a photo in an email message as well as the different ways to get photos from your camera. Next, research Windows Live Essentials and include a description of how to organize and find your pictures.

3: Researching Multiple Operating Systems
Professional
You are working as an information technology intern at a large insurance agency's headquarters. Because the company is thinking about upgrading all its computers, your boss has tasked you with researching different operating systems. Using the Internet, a library, or other research facility, write a brief report on the Windows, Mac OS, and Linux operating systems. Describe the systems, pointing out their similarities and differences. Discuss the advantages and disadvantages of each. Finally, tell which operating system you would purchase and explain why.

> Found within the Cases & Places exercises, the **Make It Personal** exercise calls on students to create an open-ended project that relates to their personal lives.

LEARN ONLINE
Reinforce what you learned in this chapter with games, exercises, training, and many other online activities and resources.

Student Companion Site: Reinforce chapter terms and concepts using review questions, flash cards, practice tests, and interactive learning games, such as a crossword puzzle. These and other online activities and resources are available at no additional cost on www.cengagebrain.com <http://www.cengagebrain.com> . Visit www.cengage.com/ct/studentdownload <http://www.cengage.com/ct/studentdownload> for detailed instructions about accessing the resources available at the Student Companion Site.

Microsoft® WINDOWS 8

INTRODUCTORY

1 Getting Started with Windows 8

Objectives

You will have mastered the material in this chapter when you can:

- Describe Windows 8
- Explain the following terms: operating system, server, workstation, and user interface
- Differentiate among the various editions of Windows 8
- Use a touch screen and perform basic mouse operations
- Start Windows 8 and sign in to an account
- Identify the objects on the Windows 8 Start screen
- Run an app
- Navigate within an app
- Display the Charms bar
- Switch between apps
- Move and resize a tile
- Search for an app or a file
- Install an app
- Use Windows Help
- Sign out of an account and shut down the computer

1 | Getting Started with Windows 8

What Is Windows 8?

An **operating system** is a computer program (set of instructions) that coordinates all the activities of computer hardware, such as memory, storage devices, and printers, and provides the capability for you to communicate with the computer.

Windows 8 is the newest version of Microsoft Windows, which is a popular and widely used operating system. The Windows operating system simplifies the process of working with documents and apps by organizing the manner in which you interact with the computer. Windows is used to run apps. An **app** (short for application) consists of programs that are designed to make users more productive and/or assist them with personal tasks, such as word processing or browsing the web.

The new Windows 8 interface begins with the **Start screen**, which shows tiles (shown in Figure 1–3 on page WIN 7). A **tile** is a shortcut to an app or other content. The tiles on the Start screen include installed apps that you use regularly. From the Start screen, you can choose which apps to run using a touch screen, mouse, or other input device.

Windows commonly is used on desktops, laptops, and workstations. A **workstation** is a computer connected to a server. A **server** is a computer that controls access to the hardware and software on a network and provides a centralized storage area for programs, data, and information. Figure 1–1 illustrates a simple computer network consisting of a server, three workstations, and a printer connected to the server.

Windows is easy to use and can be customized to fit individual needs. The operating system simplifies working with documents and programs, transferring data between documents, interacting with the different components of the computer, and using the computer to access information on the Internet or an intranet. The **Internet** is a worldwide group of connected computer networks that allows public access to information about thousands of subjects and gives users the ability to use this information, send messages, and obtain products and services. An **intranet** is an internal network that uses Internet technologies.

Windows 8 has improved memory management so that it runs faster and more efficiently than Windows 7, the previous version of the Windows operating system. The user interface also has been enhanced to create a more user-friendly and customizable experience. Several other improvements over previous versions of Windows make Windows 8 a suitable choice for all users.

This book demonstrates how to use Windows 8 to control the computer and communicate with other computers, both on a network and the Internet. In Chapter 1, you will learn about Windows and how to use some of its basic features.

Figure 1–1

Overview

As you read this chapter, you will learn how to use the Windows by performing these general tasks:

- Start Windows and sign in to an account
- Work with the Start screen
- Use the Charms bar
- Run and switch between apps
- Use the Help system to answer questions
- Sign out of an account and turn off the computer

Multiple Editions of Windows 8

Windows 8 is available in multiple editions. The first, Windows 8, is simplified and designed primarily for home and small office users. The next version is **Windows 8 Pro**, which is designed for businesses and technical professionals. **Windows 8 Enterprise** has the same features as Windows 8 Pro but is designed for large enterprises. Finally, **Windows 8 RT** is designed for devices that support the ARM (Advanced RISC Machine) architecture, such as tablets and other mobile devices.

ARM-based devices typically are less powerful than traditional desktops or laptops and usually have longer battery life. Windows 8 RT can be preinstalled on any device that supports the ARM architecture.

For a PC, minimum system requirements specify that the processor is 1 GHz or faster, random access memory (RAM) is at least 1 GB (for 32-bit systems) or 2 GB (for 64-bit systems), the hard drive has at least 16 GB available space, and the video card supports DirectX 9 graphics with WDDM (Windows Display Driver Model) 1.0 or higher driver.

Windows can be customized using a Microsoft account. When you add a Microsoft account, you can sign in to the account and then sync (synchronize) your information with all of your Windows devices. This allows you to set your email configuration settings, for example, and then sync those settings with your other devices. When you sign in to your Microsoft account with another Windows device, your settings will appear the same as they do on your other Windows 8 devices.

For laptops and other devices dependent on batteries, Windows 8 includes improved power management features to ensure longer battery life by suspending background apps, putting devices into low-powered modes sooner, and reducing RAM usage.

Navigating Using Touch or a Mouse

Windows 8 provides touch support. With touch, you can use your fingers to control how Windows functions. For example, you can swipe your finger from the right to display the Charms bar. (Charms are discussed in greater detail later in this chapter.) Touch also allows Windows 8 to work on devices such as smartphones and tablets.

Using a Touch Screen

Windows users who have computers or devices with touch screen capability can interact with the screen using gestures. A **gesture** is a motion you make on a touch screen with the tip of one or more fingers or your hand. Touch screens are convenient because they do not require a separate device for input. Table 1–1 presents common ways to interact with a touch screen.

Table 1–1 Touch Screen Gestures

Motion	Description	Common Uses
Tap	Quickly touch and release one finger one time.	Activate a link. Press a button. Run an app.
Double-tap	Quickly touch and release one finger two times.	Run a program or app. Zoom in (make the screen contents larger) at the location of the double tap.

Press and hold	Press and hold one finger until an action occurs.	Display a shortcut menu (immediate access to allowable actions). Activate a mode enabling you to move an item with one finger to a new location.
Drag	Press and hold one finger on an object and then move the finger to the new location.	Move an item around the screen. Scroll.
Swipe	Press and hold one finger and then move the finger horizontally or vertically on the screen.	Select an object. Swipe from edge to display a bar such as the Charms bar, App bar, and Navigation bar (all discussed later).
Stretch	Move two fingers apart.	Zoom in (make the screen contents larger).
Pinch	Move two fingers together.	Zoom out (make the screen contents smaller).

Using an On-Screen Keyboard

When using touch, you can access an on-screen keyboard that allows you to enter data using your fingers. To display the on-screen keyboard, tap or click the Touch Keyboard button on the taskbar. You tap a key on the keyboard to enter data or manipulate what you see on the screen. Figure 1–2 displays the on-screen keyboard.

Figure 1–2

Using a Mouse

Windows users who do not have touch screen capabilities typically work with a mouse that has at least two buttons. For a right-handed user, the left button usually is the primary mouse button, and the right mouse button is the secondary mouse button. Left-handed people, however, can reverse the function of these buttons.

Table 1–2 explains how to perform a variety of mouse operations. Some apps also use keys in combination with the mouse to perform certain actions. For example, when you hold down the CTRL key while rolling the mouse wheel, text on the screen may become larger or smaller based on the direction you roll the wheel. The function of the mouse buttons and the wheel varies depending on the app.

Table 1–2 Mouse Operations

Operation	Mouse Action	Example
Point	Move the mouse until the pointer on the desktop is positioned on the item of choice	Position the pointer on the screen
Click	Press and release the primary mouse button, which usually is the left mouse button	Select or deselect items on the screen or run an app or app feature
Right-click	Press and release the secondary mouse button, which usually is the right mouse button	Display a shortcut menu
Double-click	Quickly press and release the left mouse button two times without moving the mouse	Run an app or app feature
Triple-click	Quickly press and release the left mouse button three times without moving the mouse	Select a paragraph
Drag	Point to an item, hold down the left mouse button, move the item to the desired location on the screen, and then release the left mouse button	Move an object from one location to another or draw pictures
Right-drag	Point to an item, hold down the right mouse button, move the item to the desired location on the screen, and then release the right mouse button	Display a shortcut menu after moving an object from one location to another
Rotate wheel	Roll the wheel forward or backward	Scroll vertically (up and down)
Free-spin wheel	Whirl the wheel forward or backward so that it spins freely on its own	Scroll through many pages in seconds
Press wheel	Press the wheel button while moving the mouse	Scroll continuously
Tilt wheel	Press the wheel toward the right or left	Scroll horizontally (left and right)
Press thumb button	Press the button on the side of the mouse with your thumb	Move forward or backward through webpages and/or control media, games, and so forth

BTW
Minimizing Wrist Injury
Computer users frequently switch between the keyboard and the mouse during a word processing session; such switching strains the wrist. To help prevent wrist injury, minimize switching. For instance, if your fingers already are on the keyboard, use keyboard keys to scroll. If your hand already is on the mouse, use the mouse to scroll. If you are using touch input, minimize switching between touch input and the keyboard or mouse.

Scrolling

A **scroll bar** is a horizontal or vertical bar that appears when the contents of an area may not be visible completely on the screen (Figure 1–3). A scroll bar contains **scroll arrows** and a **scroll box** that enable you to view areas that currently cannot be seen on the screen. Tapping or clicking the up and down scroll arrows moves the screen content up or down one line. You also can tap or click above or below the scroll box to move up or down a section, or drag the scroll box up or down to move to a specific location.

Working with Apps **WIN 13**

1
- Press and hold, and then release, or right-click the screen to display the Navigation bar (Figure 1–10).

Figure 1–10

2
- Tap or click the World weather button to display the current world weather information (Figure 1–11).

Figure 1–11

3
- After viewing the current world weather information, press and hold, and then release, or right-click the screen to display the Navigation bar (Figure 1–12).

Figure 1–12

4
- Tap or click the Home button to return to the Home screen for the Weather app (Figure 1–13).

Figure 1–13

1
- Tap, swipe, or click the lock screen (Figure 1–5) to display a sign-in screen.

Figure 1–5

2
- Tap or click the user icon (for SC Series, in this case) on the sign-in screen, which depending on settings, either will display a second sign-in screen that contains a password text box (Figure 1–6) or will display the Windows Start screen.

Q&A

Why do I not see a user icon?
Your computer may require you to type a user name instead of tapping or clicking an icon.

What is a text box?
A text box is a rectangular box in which you type text.

Why does my screen not show a password text box?
Your account does not require a password.

Figure 1–6

WIN 10   Windows Chapter 1   Getting Started with Windows 8

3
- If Windows 8 displays a password text box, type your password in the text box and then tap or click the Submit button to sign in to your account and display the Start screen (Figure 1–7).

Q&A

Why does my Start screen look different from the one shown in Figure 1–7?

The Windows 8 Start screen is customizable, and your school or employer may have modified the screen to meet its needs. Also, your screen resolution, which affects the size of the elements on the screen, may differ from the screen resolution used in this book. Later in this chapter, you will learn how to change screen resolution.

How do I type if my tablet has no keyboard?

You can use your fingers to press keys on a keyboard that appears on the screen, called an on-screen keyboard, or you can purchase a separate physical keyboard that attaches to or wirelessly communicates with the tablet.

Figure 1–7

Exploring the Start Screen

The **Start screen** is a new addition to the Windows operating system and uses Microsoft's **Modern UI** (user interface) to display tiles that can be used to run apps. The Start screen provides a scrollable space for you to access apps that have been pinned to it (shown in Figure 1–7). In addition to running apps, you can perform tasks such as pinning apps (placing tiles) on the Start screen, moving the tiles around the Start screen, and unpinning apps (removing tiles) from the Start screen.

A tile is shown as a rectangle or square on the Start screen. Tapping or clicking a tile will run the app associated with the tile. **Live tiles** are tiles that when configured, update the tile with information while the Start screen is displayed. For example, if you configure the Weather app to your location, the tile will update with current weather conditions in your city.

Working with Apps

An app uses the entire screen by default. They work smoothly with touch and other input devices. When using the app, the **App bar** provides the primary command interface for the app. Because the app runs full screen, you will experience no distraction from any other app running at the same time and can focus on the current app and performing the task at hand.

To Run an App Using the Start Screen

The Start screen contains tiles that allow you to run apps, some of which may be stored on your computer. *Why? When you install an app, one or more tiles are added to the Start screen so that you easily can run the app.*

The following steps, which assume Windows is running, use the Start screen to run the Weather app based on a typical installation. Although the steps illustrate running the Weather app, the steps to run any app are similar.

1
- If necessary, swipe or scroll to display the Weather tile on the Start screen.
- Tap or click the Weather tile to run the Weather app (Figure 1–8).

Q&A What happens when you run an app?

Many apps, including the Weather app, appear full screen. Other apps run in the desktop using a window. A **window** is a rectangular area that displays data and information. The top of a window has a **title bar**, which is a horizontal space that contains the window's name.

Figure 1–8

2
- Tap or click the Allow button to allow the Weather app to use the current location (Figure 1–9).
- If your location cannot be detected, type your current city in the Enter Location text box, and then tap or click your city in the list that appears.

Figure 1–9

Other Ways
1. Tap or click Search charm on Charms bar, type app name in Search box, tap or click app name in results list

To Navigate within an App

To navigate within an app, you can use gestures or the scroll bar to see more of the app, or you can display the Navigation bar for an app. In the Weather app, the Navigation bar lets you move from the Home screen to other places, and even displays world weather. *Why? You may intend to travel or you may be interested in seeing the weather in a different location.*

The following steps display the current world weather information.

Using Charms

Windows includes several charms that can be used to find files, share information, display the Start screen, manipulate connected devices, and change settings. No matter where you are or what you are doing in Windows, you always are able to display the Charms bar.

To Return to the Start Screen

When you are finished using an app, returning to the Start screen allows you to perform another action, such as starting another app, in Windows. *Why? When working with Windows, you may decide to return to the Start screen in order to run another app.*

The following steps display the Start screen without exiting the Weather app.

1
- Swipe from the right or point to the upper-right corner of the screen to display the Charms bar (Figure 1–14).

Figure 1–14

2
- Tap or click the Start charm on the Charms bar to return to the Start screen (Figure 1–15 on the next page).

Figure 1–15

Other Ways

1. Press WINDOWS key
2. Click lower-left corner of screen, tap or click Start screen live preview
3. Swipe from left side of screen

Working with Apps

As discussed previously in this chapter, one way you can run an app in Windows is by clicking that app's tile on the Start screen. In addition to running apps, Windows enables you to switch between apps easily so that you can work with multiple apps at one time or exit apps when you have finished using them.

To Switch between Apps

In Windows, you can switch between apps easily. *Why?* *You may have several apps running and want to work with a different app than the one you currently are using.*

The following steps switch from the Start screen to the Weather app.

1
- Point to the upper-left corner of the screen to display the current apps running (Figure 1–16).

Figure 1–16

2
- Tap or click the Weather app live preview to switch to the Weather app (Figure 1–17).

Figure 1–17

Other Ways
1. Swipe from left side of screen

Understanding How to Exit Apps

With Windows, apps that you currently are not using run in the background. Windows automatically exits those apps that you have not used for an extended period of time. If you choose to do so, however, you can exit apps rather than allowing Windows to do it for you.

To Display the Windows Desktop

With Windows, you still can run and use traditional apps that require the use of the Windows desktop. **Why?** *The desktop provides many useful functions, and not all apps use the Modern UI.*

The step on the following page displays the Windows desktop.

1
- Press the WINDOWS key to return to the Start screen.
- Tap or click the Desktop tile to display the desktop (Figure 1–18).

Figure 1–18

The Windows 8 Desktop

Think of the Windows desktop as an electronic version of the top of your desk. You can perform tasks such as placing objects on the desktop, moving the objects around the desktop, and removing items from the desktop.

When you run an app in Windows, it may appear on the desktop. Some icons also may be displayed on the desktop. For instance, the icon for the **Recycle Bin**, the location of files that have been deleted, appears on the desktop by default. You can customize your desktop so that icons representing apps and files you use often appear on your desktop. When you run an app, that app's app button appears on the taskbar. By default, the **taskbar** appears at the bottom of the Windows desktop and displays the Internet Explorer app button, the File Explorer app button, and app buttons representing apps that currently are running. The right side of the taskbar contains the notification area, date, and time. The **notification area** contains icons designed to provide information about the current state of the computer. For example, the notification area can tell you if your virus protection is out of date, how much battery life you have remaining (if you are using a laptop), and whether you are connected to a network.

Working with Apps **WIN 19**

To Run the File Explorer

In Windows, you can use the File Explorer to view your files and organize them into folders as well as access these files and folders. *Why? If you want to move files and folders around on your hard disk, or copy or move files to or from a removable drive such as a USB flash drive, the File Explorer can help you perform these operations.*

The following step runs the File Explorer.

1
- Tap or click the File Explorer app button on the taskbar (shown in Figure 1–18) to run the File Explorer (Figure 1–19).

Figure 1–19

To Return to the Start Screen

The following steps display the Start screen.

1
- Swipe from the right or point to the upper-right corner of the screen to display the Charms bar.

2
- Tap or click the Start charm to return to the Start screen (Figure 1–20).

Figure 1–20

Other Ways

1. Press WINDOWS
2. Click upper-left corner of screen, tap or click Start screen live preview

To Move a Tile

After using the Start screen, you may decide to rearrange the tiles. ***Why?*** *You can place the apps that you use most often on the left side of the screen so that you can find them easily without having to scroll.* The following steps move the Mail tile to the lower left of the Start screen.

1
- If necessary, swipe or scroll to see the Mail tile (Figure 1–21).

Q&A What if I do not have the Mail tile on my Start screen?

Your Start screen can be different depending on the setup of your school/work computer. If you have no Mail tile, choose another tile to move.

Figure 1–21

2
- Drag the Mail tile to the lower left of the Start screen tiles to move the tile to that location (Figure 1–22).

Figure 1–22

Working with Apps **WIN 21**

To Resize a Tile

Windows allows you to change the size of your tiles on the Start screen. ***Why?*** *You can see more or less of a tile's information by resizing the tile.* To resize a tile, you press and hold, and then release, or right-click to display the App bar and then choose Smaller or Larger depending on how you want to resize the tile. You also can choose to unpin the app from the Start screen. The All apps button also is shown, which allows you to see all apps installed on your computer.

The following steps change the size of the Weather tile.

1
- Press and hold, and then release, or right-click the Weather tile to display the App bar (Figure 1–23).

Figure 1–23

WIN 22 Windows Chapter 1 Getting Started with Windows 8

2
- Tap or click the Smaller button on the App bar to change the size of the Weather tile to smaller (Figure 1–24).

Figure 1–24

3
- Right-click the Weather tile to display the App bar (Figure 1–25).

Figure 1–25

4
- Tap or click the Larger button on the App bar to change the size of the Weather tile to larger (Figure 1–26).

Figure 1–26

To Run an App Using the Search Box

The following steps use the Search box to run the Maps app based on a typical installation; however, you would follow similar steps to run any app. *Why? Sometimes an app does not appear on the Start screen, so you can find it quickly by searching.* Rather than searching for apps, you can tap or click the Files link to search for only files. You may need to ask your instructor how to run apps for your computer.

1

- Swipe from the right or point to the upper-right corner of the Start screen to display the Charms bar (Figure 1–27).

Figure 1–27

WIN 24 Windows Chapter 1 Getting Started with Windows 8

2
- Tap or click the Search charm on the Charms bar to display the Search menu (Figure 1–28).

Figure 1–28

3
- Type Maps as the search text in the Search text box, and watch the search results appear in the Apps list (Figure 1–29).

Q&A Do I need to type the complete app name or use correct capitalization?

No, you need to type just enough characters of the app name for it to appear in the Apps list. For example, you may be able to type M or Map, instead of Maps.

Figure 1–29

4
- Tap or click the app name, Maps in this case, in the search results to run the Maps app (Figure 1–30).
- If necessary, tap or click the Allow button to allow Maps to use your current location.

Figure 1–30

To Search the Internet Using a Charm

You also can use the Search charm to search the Internet. *Why? You need more information on a subject and want to search the Internet.* The following steps use Bing to search the Internet.

1
- Swipe from the right or point to the upper-right corner of the screen to display the Charms bar.
- Tap or click the Search charm on the Charms bar to display the Search menu (Figure 1–31 on the next page).

WIN 26 **Windows Chapter 1** Getting Started with Windows 8

Figure 1–31

2
- Tap or click the Bing link to display the Bing search area (Figure 1–32).

Figure 1–32

Working with Apps **WIN 27**

3
- Type `Windows 8` in the Search box and then press the ENTER key to search for websites about Windows 8 using the Bing app (Figure 1–33).

Windows 8 entered in Search box

search results for Windows 8

Figure 1–33

To Switch between Apps

The following steps switch from the Bing app to the Weather app.

1 Swipe from the right, and then to the left, or point to the upper-left corner of the screen and then move the mouse down to display the apps currently running.

2 Tap or click the Weather app's live preview to switch to the Weather app (Figure 1–34).

Weather app displayed

Figure 1–34

To Search an App Using a Charm

Using the Search charm, you can search an app when the app is open. *Why? While using the Weather app, you may want to find what the weather is for Las Vegas, as you will be vacationing there.* The following steps find information about the weather in Las Vegas.

1
- Swipe from the right or point to the upper-right corner of the screen to display the Charms bar.
- Tap or click the Search charm on the Charms bar to display the Search menu (Figure 1–35).

Figure 1–35

2
- Type `Las Vegas` in the Search box and then press the ENTER key to search for weather for cities named Las Vegas (Figure 1–36).

Working with Apps **WIN 29**

Windows Chapter 1

Figure 1–36

❸
- Tap or click the Las Vegas, Nevada, link to show weather for Las Vegas, Nevada (Figure 1–37).

Figure 1–37

Share Using a Charm

When running an app, you can use the Share charm to access the app's sharing options. For example, you could send an email message about the weather conditions for Las Vegas to your traveling companions so that they will be aware of weather and can pack accordingly.

To View Sharing Options Using a Charm

The following steps display the sharing options for the Weather app. *Why? The sharing options will show you what information you can share from an app and how you can share the information.*

1
- Swipe from the right or point to the upper-right corner of the screen to display the Charms bar (Figure 1–38).

Figure 1–38

2
- Tap or click the Share charm on the Charms bar to display sharing options (Figure 1–39).

Figure 1–39

Other Ways

1. Press WINDOWS+H

Working with Apps **WIN 31**

Free and Paid Apps

Many apps are available for Windows, which you can find using the Windows Store. Some apps are free, allowing you to download them without making a payment. Other apps require payment, so you will need to pay the fee before you can download them.

To Install an App

When using the Windows Store, you can install apps that are free or paid. *Why? You find an app that you want to use and download and install it so that it is on your computer.* The following steps download and install the Wikipedia app from the Windows Store. If you are not able to download and install apps on the computer you are using, read these steps without performing them.

1
- Swipe from the right or point to the upper-right corner of the screen to display the Charms bar and then tap or click the Start charm on the Charms bar to return to the Start screen.

2
- Tap or click the Store tile to run the Store app (Figure 1–40).

Figure 1–40

3
- If necessary, scroll to display the Wikipedia app.
- Tap or click the Wikipedia app to display the Wikipedia install options (Figure 1–41 on the next page).

Figure 1–41

4
- Tap or click the Install button to install the Wikipedia app (Figure 1–42).
- If prompted, enter your Microsoft account information to authorize the installation and then tap or click the OK button.

Figure 1–42

5

- Swipe from the right or point to the upper-right corner of the screen to display the Charms bar.
- Tap or click the Start charm on the Charms bar to return to the Start screen.
- Scroll to see the installed Wikipedia app (Figure 1–43).

Figure 1–43

Using Windows Help and Support

One of the more powerful Windows features is Windows Help and Support. **Windows Help and Support** is available when using Windows or when using any Microsoft app running under Windows.

Different Help options are offered depending upon whether you are at the Start screen or the Windows desktop. The links displayed in Help will depend on the app or location you currently are using.

To Start Windows Help and Support

The steps on the following pages start Windows Help and Support and open the Windows Help and Support window, which contains links to more information about Windows. *Why? This feature is designed to assist you in using Windows or the various apps.*

1
- Point to the upper-left corner of the screen to display the running apps (Figure 1–44).

Windows desktop live preview

Figure 1–44

2
- Tap or click the Desktop's live preview to switch to the desktop (Figure 1–45).

File Explorer window still open

desktop is displayed

Figure 1–45

Using Windows Help and Support **WIN 35**

3
- Swipe from the right or point to the upper-right corner of the screen to display the Charms bar (Figure 1–46).

Figure 1–46

4
- Tap or click the Settings charm on the Charms bar to display the Settings menu (Figure 1–47).

Figure 1–47

WIN 36   Windows Chapter 1   Getting Started with Windows 8

5

- Tap or click Help to open the Windows Help and Support window (Figure 1–48).

Figure 1–48

Other Ways

1. In the desktop, press F1

To Browse Help

Browsing Help allows you to view Help articles by tapping or clicking predefined links to assist you with finding the help you require. *Why?* You may not be certain about the topic you want to research, so you browse Help and Support to find the topic you need.

The following steps display the Getting started help link.

1

- Tap or click the Browse help link to display the Help topics (Figure 1–49).

Q&A

Why does the pointer turn into a hand?

The pointer changes to a hand when it is positioned on a link that you can click.

Why is the content in my Windows Help and Support window different?

Windows Help and Support updates regularly from the Internet. As these updates occur, you may notice content changing in Windows Help and Support.

Figure 1–49

❷
- Tap or click the Getting started link to display the Help links (Figure 1–50).

Figure 1–50

Shutting Down Windows

After completing your work with Windows, you should end your session by signing out of your account. In addition to signing out, several options are available for ending your Windows session. You can choose to sign out only, to lock the computer until you come back, to put the computer in sleep mode that saves power, or to shut down the computer as well as sign out of your account.

To Sign Out of an Account

If you are leaving the computer but do not want to turn it off, you can choose to sign out of your account. *Why? You are using a computer in the school lab and are leaving the class. The computer does not need to be shut down because a student in the following class will need to use the computer.*

The following steps sign out of an account.

❶
- Swipe from the right or point to the upper-right corner of the screen to display the Charms bar.
- Tap or click the Start charm on the Charms bar to return to the Start screen (Figure 1–51).

Figure 1–51

❷
- Tap or click the user icon to display user options (Figure 1–52).

Figure 1–52

❸
- Tap or click Sign out to sign out of your account (Figure 1–53).

Figure 1–53

Shutting Down Windows **WIN 39**

To Shut Down the Computer

When you have finished using the computer, you should shut it down. ***Why?*** *You are finished using your computer and want to shut it down to conserve power.*

The following steps shut down the computer.

1
- Tap, swipe, or click the lock screen to display the sign-in screen (Figure 1–54).

Figure 1–54

2
- Tap or click the Shut down button to display the Shut down menu (Figure 1–55).

Figure 1–55

3
- Tap or click Shut down to shut down the computer (Figure 1–56).

4
- If necessary, turn off any other devices you have connected to your computer.

![Figure showing a black screen with "Shutting down" text and a callout labeled "computer is shutting down"]

Figure 1–56

Chapter Summary

In this chapter, you have learned how to work with the Modern UI using touch and mouse operations. You started Windows, signed to in to an account, learned about the Start screen, and ran apps.

You learned how to switch between apps and use the Search box to find apps. Using Windows Help and Support, you located Help topics to learn more about Microsoft Windows. You learned how to sign out of an account and shut down the computer. The items listed below include the Windows skills you have learned in this chapter.

1. Sign In to an Account (WIN 8)
2. Run an App Using the Start Screen (WIN 11)
3. Navigate within an App (WIN 12)
4. Return to the Start Screen (WIN 15)
5. Switch between Apps (WIN 16)
6. Display the Windows Desktop (WIN 17)
7. Run the File Explorer (WIN 19)
8. Return to the Start Screen (WIN 19)
9. Move a Tile (WIN 20)
10. Resize a Tile (WIN 21)
11. Run an App Using the Search Box (WIN 23)
12. Search the Internet Using a Charm (WIN 25)
13. Search an App Using a Charm (WIN 28)
14. View Sharing Options Using a Charm (WIN 30)
15. Install an App (WIN 31)
16. Start Windows Help and Support (WIN 33)
17. Browse Help (WIN 36)
18. Sign Out of an Account (WIN 37)
19. Shut Down the Computer (WIN 39)

Chapter Summary **WIN 41**

Apply Your Knowledge

What's New in Windows 8?

Instructions: Use Windows Help and Support to perform the following tasks.

Part 1: Starting Windows Help and Support
1. Display the Windows desktop and then tap or click the Settings charm on the Charms bar. On the Settings menu, tap or click Help to open the Windows Help and Support window.
2. Tap or click the Get started link in the Windows Help and Support window.

Part 2: Exploring What's New in Windows 8
1. Tap or click the 'Get to know Windows' link to display information about the new features in Windows 8 (Figure 1–57).
    a. What are four reasons to connect to the cloud?
    b. What does it mean to snap an app?
    c. What is the function of the Devices charm?

Part 3: What's New in Security?
1. Tap or click the Browse help link.
2. If necessary, scroll to display the 'Security, privacy, and accounts' link. Tap or click the 'Security, privacy, and accounts' link to display the Security, privacy, and accounts page.
3. Tap or click the 'Security checklist for Windows' link to display the Security checklist for Windows page.
4. Answer the following questions:
    a. What is the Action Center?
    b. What is User Account Control?
    c. What is Windows Update?
5. Tap or click the Close button in the Windows Help and Support window.

Figure 1–57

Extend Your Knowledge

Extend the skills you learned in this chapter and experiment with new skills. You will use Help to complete the assignment.

Using Help

Instructions: Use Windows Help and Support to perform the following tasks.

1. Open the Windows Help and Support window.
2. Find Help about Windows shortcuts by typing `shortcuts` in the Search text box and then tapping or clicking the Search button (Figure 1–58). Tap or click the result titled 'Copy or move files and folders' and then answer the following questions:
   a. What keyboard shortcut is used to copy a file?
   b. What keyboard shortcut is used to paste a file?
   c. How do you display a shortcut menu?

Figure 1–58

3. Use Windows Help and Support to answer the following questions:
   a. What is Windows Defender?
   b. What is Windows Firewall?
   c. What settings can you control in Family Safety?
   d. What are five ways to protect your computer from viruses and other threats?
   e. What is a user account?
   f. What is the difference between a local user account and a Microsoft account?

4. Use the Search text box in Windows Help and Support to answer the following questions:
    a. How do you turn on Windows Firewall?
    b. How do you pin a program to the taskbar?
    c. How do you set up a home network in Windows?
    d. How do you add a printer?
5. The tools to solve a problem while using Windows 8 are called troubleshooters. Use Windows Help and Support to find information about troubleshooters, and answer the following questions:
    a. What problems does the Printer troubleshooter allow you to resolve?
    b. List two additional Windows 8 troubleshooters.
6. Close the Windows Help and Support window.

In the Lab

Use the guidelines, concepts, and skills presented in this chapter to increase your knowledge of Windows 8. Labs are listed in order of increasing difficulty.

Lab 1: Using Windows Help and Support

Problem: You have a few questions about using Windows and would like to answer these questions using Windows Help and Support.

Instructions: Use Windows Help and Support to perform the following tasks.

1. Open the Windows Help and Support window.
2. Use Help and Support to answer the following questions:
    a. What is a way to improve your computer's performance?
    b. How do you view your computer information?
    c. Which power plans does Windows provide?
3. Use the Search Help text box in Windows Help and Support to answer the following questions:
    a. How can you rip music from a CD using Windows Media Player?
    b. How can you play a slide show of your photos?
    c. What tools does Windows provide for fixing problems with your computer?
4. Use Windows Help and Support to obtain information about the Internet and networking (Figure 1–59).
    a. How do you set up a wireless router?
    b. How do you turn on sharing?
    c. What advice does Windows provide about fixing network adapter problems?
5. Close the Windows Help and Support window.

Continued >

In the Lab *continued*

Figure 1–59

In the Lab

Lab 2: Working with Multiple Apps

Instructions: Perform the following steps to run multiple apps with the desktop and the Search menu and then use different methods to switch among the open windows (Figure 1–60).

Figure 1–60

Part 1: Running Internet Explorer, the File Explorer, and WordPad
1. Display the Desktop and then tap or click the Internet Explorer app button on the taskbar to run Internet Explorer.
2. Tap or click the File Explorer app button to open the File Explorer window.
3. Display the Search charm and search for WordPad. Tap or click WordPad to run the WordPad app.

Part 2: Switching among the Windows
1. Press ALT+TAB to switch to the next open window.
2. Press CTRL+ALT+TAB to view the programs that are running. Press the TAB key. Tap or click the WordPad live preview to switch to the WordPad app.
3. Press CTRL+WINDOWS+TAB to view the programs that are running. Press the TAB key. Tap or click the Internet Explorer live preview to switch to Internet Explorer.

Part 3: Reporting Your Findings
1. What happens when you press ALT+TAB?
2. What is the difference between pressing ALT+TAB and CTRL+ALT+TAB?

In the Lab

Lab 3: Using Internet Explorer

Instructions: Perform the following steps to run Internet Explorer and explore a selection of websites.

Part 1: Running Internet Explorer
1. If necessary, connect to the Internet.
2. Display the desktop and then run Internet Explorer.

Part 2: Exploring the Cengage Website
1. Tap or click the web address in the address bar to select it.
2. Type cengage.com in the address bar and then press the ENTER key (Figure 1–61 on the next page).
3. Answer the following questions:
    a. What web address is displayed in the address bar?
    b. What window title appears on the title bar?
4. If necessary, swipe or scroll to view the contents of the webpage. List three links shown on this webpage.
5. Tap or click any link on the webpage. Which link did you tap or click?
6. Describe the webpage that was displayed when you tapped or clicked the link.
7. If requested by your instructor, tap or click the Print button to print the webpage.

Continued >

In the Lab *continued*

Figure 1–61

Part 3: Exploring Universal Studios: Orlando's Website
1. Tap or click the web address in the address bar to select it.
2. Type `universalorlando.com` in the address bar and then press the ENTER key.
3. What title is displayed on the title bar?
4. Swipe or scroll the webpage to view its contents. Do any graphic images display on the webpage?
5. Does the webpage include an image that is a link? (Recall that pointing to an image on a webpage and having the pointer change to a hand indicates the image is a link.) If so, describe the image.
6. Tap or click the image to display another webpage. What window title is displayed on the title bar?
7. If requested by your instructor, tap or click the Print button to print the webpage.

Part 4: Displaying Previously Displayed Webpages
1. Tap or click the Back button. What webpage is displayed?
2. Tap or click the Back button twice. What webpage is displayed?
3. Tap or click the Print button to print the webpage, if requested by your instructor.
4. Tap or click the Close button on the Internet Explorer title bar to exit Internet Explorer.

Cases and Places

Apply your creative thinking and problem-solving skills to design and implement a solution.

1: Assessing Windows 8 Compatibility
Academic
You work part-time as a lab technician in your school's computer lab. Your boss wants to upgrade several computers in the lab and has asked you to investigate. You know that the Windows 8 operating system can be installed only on computers found in the Windows 8 Hardware Compatibility List. Locate three older personal computers. Look for them in your school's computer lab, at a local business, or in your house. Use the Windows website to locate the Windows 8 Compatibility Center. Check each computer against the list and write a brief report summarizing your results.

2: Sharing Your Pictures
Personal
You recently attended your high school reunion, and your friend has asked for your help. She wants to send photos to several classmates via email messages and is not sure how best to proceed. Using Windows Help and Support and the keywords, digital pictures, locate the 'How to use Windows Photo Viewer' article. In a brief report, summarize the steps required to send a photo in an email message as well as the different ways to get photos from your camera.

3: Researching Multiple Operating Systems
Professional
You are working as an information technology intern at a large insurance agency's headquarters. Because the company is thinking about upgrading all its computers, your boss has tasked you with researching different operating systems. Using the Internet, a library, or other research facility, write a brief report on the Windows, Mac OS, and Linux operating systems. Describe the most recent version of each operating system, pointing out their similarities and differences. Discuss the advantages and disadvantages of each. Finally, tell which operating system you would purchase and explain why.

LEARN ONLINE
Reinforce what you learned in this chapter with games, exercises, training, and many other online activities and resources.

Student Companion Site: Reinforce chapter terms and concepts using review questions, flash cards, practice tests, and interactive learning games, such as a crossword puzzle. These and other online activities and resources are available at no additional cost on www.cengagebrain.com. Visit www.cengage.com/ct/studentdownload for detailed instructions about accessing the resources available at the Student Companion Site.

2 File and Folder Management

Objectives

You will have mastered the material in this chapter when you can:

- View the contents of a drive and folder using the Computer folder window
- View the properties of files and folders
- Find files and folders from a folder window
- Use Shake and Snap to manipulate windows
- View the contents of the Pictures library
- View and change the properties of a picture
- Run and use the Photos app
- View pictures as a slide show
- Zip a folder and view the contents of a zipped folder

2 File and Folder Management

Introduction

In Chapter 2, you will use Windows to create documents on the desktop and work with documents and folders in the Documents library. Windows also allows you to examine the files and folders on the computer in a variety of other ways, enabling you to choose the easiest and most accessible manner when working with a computer or mobile device. The Computer folder window and the Documents library provide two ways for you to work with files and folders. In addition, the Pictures library allows you to organize and share picture files, and the Music library allows you to organize and share your music files.

Overview

As you read this chapter, you will learn how to work with the Computer folder window, as well as the Documents, Pictures, and Music libraries, by performing these general tasks:

- Open and use the Computer folder window
- Search for files and folders
- Manage open windows
- Open and use the Pictures library
- Zip folder content
- Use the Photos app
- View pictures as a slide show

The Computer Folder Window

As noted in the previous chapter, the desktop displays the File Explorer app button. Tapping or clicking the File Explorer app button opens the File Explorer window. Using the navigation bar, you can navigate to the Computer folder that contains the storage devices that are installed on the computer. Windows uses folder windows to display the contents of the computer. A **folder window** consists of tabs at the top that display the ribbon with multiple commands, an address bar below the ribbon, a toolbar to the left of the address bar containing buttons to help you navigate your computer's folder structure, a navigation pane on the left below the toolbar, a headings bar and list area on the right below the address bar, and a status bar at the bottom of the window. Depending upon which folder or library you are viewing — Computer, Documents, Pictures, and so on — the folder window will display the toolbar options that are most appropriate for working with the contents.

> **BTW**
> **Managing Windows**
> Having multiple windows open on the desktop can intimidate some users. Consider working in a maximized window, and when you want to switch to another open window, use the Switch List to switch to that window.

To Open and Maximize the Computer Folder Window

The list area of the Computer folder window groups objects based upon the different types of devices connected to your computer. The Hard Disk Drives group contains the Local Disk (C:) icon that represents the hard disk on the computer. The **hard disk** is where you can store files and folders. Storing data on a hard disk is more convenient than storing data on a USB flash drive because the hard disk is readily available and generally has more available storage space. A computer always will have at least one hard disk, which normally is designated as drive C. On the computer represented by the Computer folder window in Figure 2–1, the icon consists of an image of a hard disk and a **disk label**, or title, Local Disk, and a drive letter (C:). The disk label can change and may differ depending upon the name assigned to the hard disk. For example, some people label their hard disks based upon usage; therefore, it could be called PRIMARY (C:), where PRIMARY is the label given to the hard disk as it is the drive that houses the operating system and main apps.

The following steps open and maximize the Computer folder window. *Why? This will allow you to view the content in its entirety.*

1
- If necessary, sign in to your Windows account.
- Display the Start screen.
- Display the desktop.

2
- Tap or click the File Explorer app button to run the File Explorer app.

3
- Tap or click Computer in the navigation pane to open the Computer folder window. If necessary, maximize the Computer folder window (Figure 2–1).

Figure 2–1

To Display Properties for the Local Disk (C:) Drive in the Details Pane

The details pane of a folder window displays the properties of devices, apps, files, and folders, which all are considered to be objects by Windows. Every object in Windows has properties that describe the object. A **property** is a characteristic of an object such as the amount of storage space on a storage device or the number of items in a folder. The properties of each object will differ, and in some cases, you can change the properties of an object. *Why? For example, in the Local Disk (C:) properties, you could check the file system being used on the drive using the File system property. To determine the drive's capacity, you would view the Total size property.* The following steps display the properties for the Local Disk (C:) in the details pane of the Computer folder window.

❶
- Tap or click the Local Disk (C:) icon to select the hard disk and select the Local Disk (C:) (Figure 2–2).

Figure 2–2

❷
- Tap or click View on the ribbon to display the View tab (Figure 2–3).

Figure 2–3

3
- Tap or click the Details pane button to display the details pane (Figure 2–4).

🔍 **Experiment**

See what properties are displayed for the other disks and devices shown. Tap or click each one and note what properties appear in the details pane. Return to the Local Disk (C:) when you are done.

Q&A | Why do the properties of my local disk differ from those in the figure?
The size and contents of your disk will be different from the one in the figure. As a result, the properties of the disk also will be different. Depending upon what has been installed on the disk and how it is formatted, the Space used, Space free, Total size, and File system properties will vary.

Figure 2–4

Other Ways

1. Tap or click Local Disk (C:) icon, press ALT+SHIFT+P

To Display the Local Disk (C:) Properties Dialog Box

The properties shown in the details pane are just a few of the properties of drive C. In fact, the details pane is used to highlight the most popular properties of a hard disk: how much space is used, how much space is free, the size of the disk, and how the disk is formatted. You can display more detailed information about the hard disk.

Why? *You would like to view information about the hard disk, such as the disk capacity, and perform other actions to help increase the disk's performance.* The Tools sheet, accessible by tapping or clicking the Tools tab, allows you to check for errors on the hard disk, defragment the hard disk, or back up the hard disk. The Hardware sheet allows you to view a list of all disk drives, troubleshoot disk drives that are not working properly, and display the properties for each disk drive. The Sharing sheet allows you to share the contents of a hard disk with other computer users. To protect a computer from unauthorized access, however, sharing the hard disk is not recommended. The Security sheet displays the security settings for the drive, such as user permissions. The Previous Versions sheet allows you to work with copies of your hard disk that are created when using backup utilities or from automatic saves. Finally, the Quota sheet can be used to see how much space is being used by various user accounts. Other tabs might be displayed in the Local Disk (C:) Properties dialog box on your computer.

The following step displays the Properties dialog box for the Local Disk (C:) drive.

WIN 54 Windows Chapter 2 File and Folder Management

1

- Tap or click the Properties button (Computer tab | Location group) to display the Local Disk (C:) Properties dialog box (Figure 2–5).

Figure 2–5

Other Ways

1. Press and hold, then release or right-click Local Disk (C:) icon, tap or click Properties on shortcut menu
2. Select drive icon, press ALT+ENTER

To Close the Local Disk (C:) Properties Dialog Box

Now that you have reviewed the Local Disk (C:) Properties dialog box, you should close it. The following step closes the dialog box. *Why? Closing the dialog box lets you continue working in the Computer folder window without the dialog box being displayed.*

1

- Tap or click the OK button (Local Disk (C:) Properties dialog box) to close it (Figure 2–6).

Figure 2–6

Other Ways

1. Tap or click Cancel button
2. Tap or click Close button
3. Press ESC

To Switch Folders Using the Address Bar

Why? Found in all folder windows, the address bar lets you know which folder you are viewing. A useful feature of the address bar is its capability to allow you to switch to different folder windows by tapping or clicking the arrows preceding or following the folder names. Tapping or clicking the arrow to the right of the computer icon, for example, displays a menu containing options for showing the desktop in a folder window, switching to the Computer folder, the Recycle Bin, the Control Panel, and other locations and folders that can vary from computer to computer. The following steps change the folder window from displaying the Computer folder to displaying the desktop and then return to the Computer folder.

1

- Tap or click the arrow to the right of the computer icon on the address bar to display a menu that contains folder switching commands (Figure 2–7). Depending upon your computer's configuration, the list of commands might differ.

Figure 2–7

2

- Tap or click Desktop on the menu to switch to viewing the contents of the desktop in the folder window (Figure 2–8).

Q&A Why do icons appear in this folder window that are not displayed on the desktop?

Although these icons are not displayed on the desktop, Microsoft provides you with convenient access to Libraries, the Control Panel, and the Network folder window (if applicable) by placing these icons in the Desktop folder window.

Figure 2–8

3

- Tap or click the 'Back to Computer' button to return to the Computer folder (Figure 2–9 on the next page).

WIN 56　Windows Chapter 2　File and Folder Management

Figure 2–9

To View the Contents of a Drive

In addition to viewing the contents of the Computer folder, you can view the contents of drives and folders. In fact, the contents of any folder or drive on the computer will be displayed in a folder window. By default, Windows uses the active window to display the contents of a newly opened drive or folder. The following step displays the contents of drive C in the active window. *Why? You should know the contents of the drive so that you can see where your information is stored.*

1

- Double-tap or double-click the Local Disk (C:) icon in the Computer folder window to display the contents of the Local Disk (C:) drive (Figure 2–10).

Q&A Why do I see different folders?
The contents of the Local Disk (C:) window that appear on your computer can differ from the contents shown in Figure 2–10 because each computer has its own folders, apps, and documents.

Figure 2–10

Other Ways

1. Press and hold, then release or right-click Local Disk (C:), tap or click Open on shortcut menu
2. Tap or click Local Disk (C:), press ENTER

To Preview the Properties of a Folder

Why? When you move the pointer over a folder icon, a preview of the folder properties will display in a ScreenTip. A **ScreenTip** is a brief description that appears when you position the pointer over an object on the screen. ScreenTips do not appear for every object, but when they do, they provide useful information. The properties typically consist of the date and time created, the folder size, and the name of the folder. The Windows folder in the Local Disk (C:) window contains apps and files necessary for the operation of the Windows operating system. As such, you should exercise caution when working with the contents of the Windows folder, because changing the contents of the folder might cause the operating system to stop working correctly.

The following step shows a ScreenTip displaying the properties of the Windows folder.

1
- Point to the Windows folder icon to display a ScreenTip displaying the properties of the Windows folder (Figure 2–11).

Figure 2–11

To Display Properties for the Windows Folder in the Details Pane

Just like with drives, some properties of folders can be displayed in the details pane. The following step displays the properties for the Windows folder in the details pane of the Computer folder window.

1
- Tap or click the Windows folder icon to display the properties in the details pane (Figure 2–12).

Figure 2–12

To Display All of the Properties of the Windows Folder

Why? *If you want to see all of the properties for the Windows folder, you will need to display the Properties dialog box.* The following steps display the Properties dialog box for the Windows folder.

1
- Press and hold, then release, or right-click the Windows folder icon to display a shortcut menu (Figure 2–13). (The commands on your shortcut menu might differ.)

Figure 2–13

2
- Tap or click Properties on the shortcut menu to display the Windows Properties dialog box (Figure 2–14).

3
- Tap or click the OK button (Windows Properties dialog box) to close it.

Experiment
Tap or click the various tabs in the Windows Properties dialog box to see the different properties available for a folder.

Q&A Why might I want to look at the properties of a folder?

When you are working with folders, you might need to look at folders' properties to make changes, such as configuring a folder for sharing over a network or hiding folders from users who do not need access to them.

Why are the tabs of the Windows folder properties different from the Local Disk (C:) properties?

Drives, folders, and files have different properties and, therefore, need different tabs. A folder's Properties dialog box typically shows the General, Sharing, Security, and Previous Versions tabs; however, depending upon your Windows 8 edition and installed apps, they may differ. The Properties dialog box always will have the General tab, although its displays also may differ.

Figure 2–14

To View the Contents of a Folder

The following step opens the Windows folder so that you can view its contents. *Why? You will be able see what sort of files your operating system installed.*

1
- Double-tap or double-click the Windows folder icon to display the contents of the Windows folder (Figure 2–15).

Figure 2–15

Other Ways

1. Press and hold, then release, or right-click Windows folder, tap or click Open on shortcut menu
2. Tap or click Windows folder, press ENTER

Searching for Files and Folders

The majority of objects displayed in the Windows folder, as shown in Figure 2–15, are folder icons. Folder icons always are displayed in alphabetical order at the top of the file list in a folder window, before the icons for apps or files.

Folders such as the Windows folder can contain many files and folders. When you want to find a particular file or folder but do not know where it is located, you can use the **Search box** to find the file or folder quickly. When you are in a folder, the Search box displays the word, Search, plus the folder name. For example, in the Windows folder, the Search box contains the text, Search Windows. As soon as you start typing, the window updates to show search results that match what you are typing. As Windows is searching for files or folders that match your search criteria, you will see a searching message displayed in the list area, an animated circle attached to the pointer, and an animated progress bar on the address bar, which provides

BTW
Hidden Files and Folders
Hidden files and folders usually are placed on your computer's hard disk by software vendors such as Microsoft and often are critical to the operation of their apps. Rarely will you need to designate a file or folder as hidden. You should not delete a hidden file or folder, as doing so might interrupt how or whether an app works. By default, hidden files and folders are not displayed in a file listing.

live feedback as to how much of the search has been completed. When searching is complete, you will see a list of all the items that match your search criteria.

If you know only a portion of a file's name and can specify where the known portion of the name should appear, you can use an asterisk in the name to represent the unknown characters. For example, if you know a file starts with the letters MSP, you can type `msp*` in the Search box. All files that begin with the letters, msp, regardless of what characters follow, will be displayed. With Windows 8's powerful search capabilities, however, you would get the same results if you did not include the asterisk. If you want to search for all files with a particular extension, you can use the asterisk to substitute for the name of the files. For example, to find all the text files with the extension .rtf, you would type `*.rtf` in the Search box. Windows will find all the files with the .rtf extension.

To Search for a File and Folder in a Folder Window

The following step uses the Search box to search the Windows folder for all the objects that contain the letters, aero, in the file name. ***Why?*** *Sometimes you may forget where a file is stored. Knowing how to search can help you find files faster.*

1

- Type `aero` in the Search box to search for all files and folders that match the search criteria (Figure 2–16).

Q&A How can I stop a search while it is running?

If you decide to stop a search before it is finished running, tap or click the Stop button (the small x) that appears next to the Search box.

Figure 2–16

To Clear the Search Box

When you finish searching, you can end the search by clearing the Search box. The following step clears the Search box. **Why?** *You clear the Search box so that you can resume normal navigation of the folder you are viewing.*

1

- Tap or click the Stop button (denoted with an x in the Search box) to clear the Search box and redisplay all files and folders in the Windows folder (Figure 2–17).

Figure 2–17

To Open Windows

In this chapter, you have been working with one window open. Windows allows you to open many more windows depending upon the amount of RAM that is installed on the computer. Too many open windows on the desktop, however, can become difficult to use and manage. Windows provides several tools for managing open windows. You already have used one tool, maximizing a window. When you maximize a window, it occupies the entire screen and cannot be confused with other open windows.

Sometimes, it is important to have multiple windows appear on the desktop simultaneously. Windows offers simple commands that allow you to arrange multiple windows in specific ways. The following sections describe the ways that you can manage multiple open windowsv. The following steps open another File Explorer window.

1 Press and hold, then release or right-click the File Explorer app button.

2 Tap or click File Explorer on the shortcut menu to open another File Explorer window.

3 Tap or click the Pictures folder to display its contents.

To Use Shake to Minimize and Restore All Windows

Shake lets you minimize all windows except the active window and then restore all those windows by shaking the title bar of the active window. The following steps use Shake to minimize all windows except the Music library and then restore those windows.

1
- Tap or click the title bar of the Pictures library window, and then shake the title bar (drag the title bar back and forth in short, swift motions several times) to minimize all windows except the Pictures library (Figure 2–18).

Figure 2–18

2
- Tap or click the title bar of the Pictures library window, and then shake the title bar to restore all the windows (Figure 2–19).

Figure 2–19

To Use Snap to Maximize Windows

Why? *Sometimes you want to see a larger portion of a window.* Snap allows you to maximize a window by dragging its title bar to the top of the screen. The following steps maximize the Pictures library window.

1
- Press and hold or click the title bar of the Pictures library window.

2
- Drag the Pictures library window to the top of the screen to maximize the Pictures library window (Figure 2–20).

Q&A Can only Snap be used to maximize windows?

No. If you drag a window's title bar to the right side of the screen, the window will resize to fill the right half of the screen. If you drag the title bar to the left side of the screen, the window will resize to fill only the left half of the screen.

Figure 2–20

To Use the Show Desktop Button to Minimize All Windows

Why? *You need to access an app or file that is on the desktop, so you minimize all open windows so that you can access it.* The following step minimizes all windows to show the desktop.

1
- Tap or click the Show Desktop button on the taskbar to minimize all windows (Figure 2–21 on the next page).

Figure 2–21

To Restore a Window

Why? *To work with one of the windows, you first must restore it.* You can use the File Explorer app button on the taskbar and live preview to switch to the Pictures library window.

The following steps switch to the Pictures library window; however, the steps are the same for any app currently displayed as an app button on the taskbar.

1
- Press and hold or point to the File Explorer app button on the taskbar to see a live preview of the open File Explorer windows or the window title(s) of the open window(s), depending on your computer's configuration (Figure 2–22).

Figure 2–22

2
- Tap or click the live preview of the Pictures library window to restore the window (Figure 2–23).

Q&A What happens if I tap or click the wrong window?

Tap or click the remaining windows until the Pictures window is displayed in the foreground.

Figure 2–23

Other Ways

1. Press ALT+TAB until Pictures folder window is selected, release ALT key

The Pictures Library

You can organize your pictures and share them with others using the Pictures library. By putting all your pictures in the Pictures library, you always will know where to find them. When you save pictures from a digital camera, scanner, or the Internet, they are saved to the Pictures library by default. More specifically, they are saved to the My Pictures folder. The My Pictures folder is part of the Pictures library and is set as the default save location to be used when working with the library. Each library has a default save location; the default save location for the Documents library is the My Documents folder.

Windows 8 also includes the Photos app. The **Photos app** is used when you download pictures from your digital camera. Unlike the Pictures library, files saved in the Photos app are stored in the app and not the My Pictures folder. You can use the Photos app to work with your pictures even if they are stored in the Pictures library.

Using the Pictures library allows you to organize pictures, preview pictures, share your pictures with others, display your pictures as a slide show, print your pictures, attach your pictures to email messages, or save your pictures on an optical disc. You will work with a few of the options now, and the rest will be covered in a later chapter when multimedia files are covered in greater depth.

Many different formats are available for picture files. Some pictures have an extension of .bmp to indicate that they are bitmap files. Other pictures may have the .gif extension, which indicates that they are saved in the Graphics Interchange Format. Too many file types exist to mention them all; however, some common types include .bmp, .jpg, .gif, .png, and .tif.

When working with pictures, you should be aware that most pictures that you did not create yourself, including other multimedia files, are copyrighted. A **copyright** means that a picture belongs to the person who created it. The pictures that come with Windows are part of Windows, and you are allowed to use them; however, they are not yours. You can use them only according to the rights given to you by Microsoft. Pictures that you take using your digital camera are yours because you created them. Before using pictures and other multimedia files, you should be aware of any copyrights associated with them, and you should know whether you are allowed to use them for your intended purpose.

Item Check Boxes

As you saw in the Local Disk (C:) folder window (Figure 2–12 on page WIN 57), when an item is selected, you clearly can see the item check box for that item. By tapping or clicking the item check box for several items, you can select them for your use. For example, you can copy files or folders from one location to another.

To Search for Pictures

Why? *You want to copy three files (img0, img2, and img4) from the Windows folder to the Pictures library, but you have to find these files first.* Because the three files all have the .jpg extension, you can search for them using an asterisk (*) in place of the number in the name, as discussed earlier in this chapter. The following steps open the Windows folder window and display the icons for the files you want to copy.

1
- Restore the Windows folder window, and, if necessary, maximize it.

2
- Type `img*.jpg` in the Search box and then press the ENTER key to search for all files that begin with img and have a .jpg file extension.

3
- If necessary, scroll down the middle pane of the Windows folder window until the icons for the img0, img2, and img4 files are visible (Figure 2–24). If one or more of these files are not available, select any of the other picture files.

Figure 2–24

To Copy Files to the Pictures Library

A method you can use to copy a file or folder is the **copy and paste** method. When you **copy** a file, you place a copy of the file in a temporary storage area of the computer called the **Clipboard**. When you **paste** the file, Windows copies it from the Clipboard to the location you specify, giving you two copies of the same file.

Why? *Because the search results include the pictures you were looking for, you now can select the files and then copy them to the Pictures library.* Once the three files have been copied to the Pictures library, the files will be stored in both the My Pictures folder (the default save location) and Windows folder on drive C. Copying and moving files are common tasks when working with Windows. If you want to move a file instead of copy a file, you use the Cut button on the ribbon to move the file to the Clipboard and the Paste command to copy the file from the Clipboard to the new location. When the paste is complete, the files are moved into the new folder and no longer are stored in the original folder.

The following steps copy the img0, img2, and img4 files from the Windows folder to the Pictures library.

1
- Tap or click the item check boxes for the img0, img2, and img4 pictures to select the files (Figure 2–25). If you do not see the item check boxes to the left of the image names, tap or click the 'Item check boxes' check box (View tab | Show/hide group).

Q&A Are copying and moving the same?

No. When you copy a file, it is located in both the place to which it was copied and in the place from which it was copied. When you move a file, it is located only in the location to which it was moved.

Figure 2–25

WIN 68 Windows Chapter 2 File and Folder Management

2
- Tap or click Home on the ribbon to display the Home tab.
- Tap or click the Copy button (Home tab | Clipboard group) to copy the files to the Clipboard (Figure 2–26).

Figure 2–26

3
- Make the Pictures library the active window (Figure 2–27).

Figure 2–27

4
- Tap or click Home on the ribbon to display the Home tab.
- Tap or click the Paste button (Home tab | Clipboard group) to paste the files in the Pictures library (Figure 2–28).

Figure 2–28

Other Ways

1. Select file icons, press and hold, then release, or right-click, tap or click Copy on shortcut menu; display window where you want to store files, press and hold, then release, or right-click, tap or click Paste on shortcut menu

2. Select file icons, press CTRL+C, display window where you want to store files, press CTRL+V

To Close the Search Results Window

You no longer need the Search Results window open, so you can close it. Whenever you are not using a window, it is a good idea to close it so as not to clutter your desktop. The following steps close the Search Results window.

1 Display the Search Results window.

2 Close the Search Results window.

To Create a Folder in the Pictures Library

Why? When you have several related files stored in a folder with a number of unrelated files, you might want to create a folder to contain the related files so that you can find and reference them easily. To reduce clutter and improve the organization of files in the Pictures library, you will create a new folder in the Pictures library and then move the pictures you copied into the new folder. The following steps create the Backgrounds folder in the Pictures library.

WIN 70 Windows Chapter 2 File and Folder Management

1
- Tap or click the New folder button on the Quick Access Toolbar to create a new folder (Figure 2–29).

Figure 2–29

2
- Type `Backgrounds` in the new folder's text box and then press the ENTER key to assign the name to the new folder (Figure 2–30).

Figure 2–30

Other Ways

1. Right-click, point to New, tap or click Folder on shortcut menu
2. Tap or click New folder button (Home tab | New group)

The Pictures Library **WIN 71**

To Move Multiple Files into a Folder

Why? *After you create the Backgrounds folder in the Pictures library, the next step is to move the three picture files into the folder.* The following steps move the img0, img2, and img4 files into the Backgrounds folder.

1

- Tap or click the check box for the Backgrounds folder to deselect the folder.
- Tap or click the item check boxes for the img0, img2, and img4 pictures to select the files (Figure 2–31).

Figure 2–31

2

- Drag the selected icons to the Backgrounds folder and then release to move the files to the Backgrounds folder (Figure 2–32).

Figure 2–32

Other Ways

1. Drag icons individually to folder icon
2. Press and hold, then release, or right-click icon, tap or click Cut on shortcut menu; press and hold, then release, or right-click folder icon, tap or click Paste on shortcut menu

To Refresh the Image on a Folder

Why? *After moving the three files into the Backgrounds folder, it still appears as an empty open folder icon.* To replace the empty folder icon with a live preview of the three files stored in the Backgrounds folder (img0, img2, and img4), the Pictures library must be refreshed. The following steps refresh the Pictures library to display the live preview for the Backgrounds folder.

1
- Press and hold, then release, or right-click any open part of the list area to display a shortcut menu (Figure 2–33).

Figure 2–33

2
- Tap or click Refresh on the shortcut menu to refresh the list area (Figure 2–34).

Figure 2–34

To View and Change the Properties of a Picture

As mentioned earlier in the chapter, in Windows, all objects have properties. You already have explored the properties of a drive, and now you will review the properties of a picture. Picture properties include the Size, Title, Authors, State, Date taken, Tags, Rating, and Dimensions. State refers to whether or not the picture is shared with other users on the computer. Date taken refers to the date the person created the picture.

Why? *Tags are keywords you associate with a picture file to aid in its classification. For example, you could tag a family photo with the names of the people in the photo.* When you create a tag, it should be meaningful. For example, if you have pictures from a family vacation at the beach and you add the title, vacation, you later will be able to find the file using the tag, vacation, in a search. Be aware that you can search only for tags that you already have created. If your family vacation photo was saved as photo1.jpg and tagged with the tag, vacation, you will not find it by searching for the word, beach, as it is not part of the name or tag. Rating refers to the ranking, in stars, that you assign to a picture. You can rate a picture from zero to five stars. Date taken, Tags, and Rating all can be changed using the details pane. Because you do not know when the Background pictures were created, you will change only the Tags and Rating properties. The following steps display and change the Tags and Rating properties of the Monet image in the Backgrounds folder.

1

- Display the contents of the Backgrounds folder.
- Tap or click the img4 icon to select it (Figure 2–35).

Figure 2–35

2

- Tap or click the 'Add a tag' text box in the details pane to activate it (Figure 2–36).

Figure 2–36

WIN 74 Windows Chapter 2 File and Folder Management

3

- Type `Majestic Scene` in the text box to create a tag for the picture (Figure 2–37).

Figure 2–37

4

- Tap or click the third star next to the Rating heading in the details pane to assign a three-star rating to the picture (Figure 2–38).

Figure 2–38

5

- Tap or click the Save button in the details pane to save the changes to the Tags and Rating properties (Figure 2–39).

Figure 2-39

> **Other Ways**
> 1. Press and hold, then release, or right-click icon, tap or click Properties, tap or click Details tab, tap or click third star next to Rating, enter text next to Tags, tap or click OK button

To View a Picture in the Photos App

Why? You can view the images in a folder in the Photos app or as a slide show. The **Photos app** allows you to view, print, burn, send via email, and open the pictures in your Pictures library. You can view pictures individually or as part of a slide show.

The following steps display the img2 picture in the Backgrounds folder in the Photos app.

1
- Select the img2 picture.
- Double-tap or double-click the icon to display the picture in the Photos app (Figure 2-40).

Figure 2-40

WIN 76 Windows Chapter 2 File and Folder Management

2
- After viewing the picture, display the desktop (Figure 2–41).

Figure 2–41

To View Your Pictures as a Slide Show

In Windows, you can view your pictures as a **slide show**, which displays each image in the folder in a presentation format on the computer screen. The slide show automatically will display one picture at a time while everything else on the desktop is hidden from sight. The slide show allows you to select whether the pictures will loop in order or will be shuffled to appear in random order. You also can select the speed at which the pictures are displayed, pause the slide show, and exit the slide show. The following steps view the images in the Backgrounds folder as a slide show.

1
- Tap or click the Slide show button (Picture Tools Manage tab | View group) to view the selected files as a slide show (Figure 2–42).

2
- Watch the show for a few seconds while the pictures change.

Q&A Can I change the slide show speed?

Yes, you can press and hold, then release, or right-click and then select speeds of Slow, Medium, and Fast on the shortcut menu.

The Pictures Library **WIN 77**

[Figure showing slide show running with daisy image]

Figure 2-42

To End a Slide Show

When you are done viewing the slide show, the next step is to end it. The following step ends the slide show.

1
- Press the ESC key to end the slide show (Figure 2-43).

[Figure showing Backgrounds window with slide show ended]

Figure 2-43

Zipping Files and Folders

Sometimes when working with files, you may need to send them via email, post them online, or even transfer them to another computer. If the files are large or numerous, you can make it easier to manage by zipping the files. Zipping a file creates a **zipped file** that will contain compressed copies of the files. You also can zip folders so that your zipped file has a copy of your folder in it.

To Zip a Folder

Why? You want to send the pictures to a friend via an email message, but you want to attach only one file, not three separate ones. The following step zips the Backgrounds folder.

1
- Navigate to the Pictures library.
- If necessary, select the Backgrounds folder.
- Click Share on the ribbon to display the Share tab.
- Tap or click the Zip button (Share tab | Send group) to create a zipped file (Figure 2–44). Press the ENTER key to accept the file name Windows gave to the file.

Figure 2–44

To View the Contents of a Zipped Folder

Why? *You want to verify that the files are in the zipped folder before you share it.* You can open a zipped folder and then view the contents as if you were browsing a regular folder. The following steps display the contents of the Backgrounds zipped folder.

1

- Double-tap or double-click the Backgrounds zipped folder icon to display the contents of the zipped folder (Figure 2–45).

Figure 2–45

2

- Double-tap or double-click the Backgrounds folder to display the contents of the folder (Figure 2–46).

Figure 2–46

Other Ways

1. Right-click or press and hold folder, tap or point to Send on shortcut menu, tap or click Compressed (zipped) folder command

To Delete a Folder from the Pictures Library

To return the Pictures library to its original state, you will delete the Backgrounds folder and the Backgrounds zipped folder. The following steps delete the Backgrounds folder and the Backgrounds zipped folder.

1. Navigate to the Pictures library.
2. Select the Backgrounds folder, display the Home tab, and then tap or click the Delete button (Home tab | Organize group) to delete the Backgrounds folder.
3. Select the Backgrounds zipped folder, display the Home tab, and then tap or click the Delete button (Home tab | Organize group) to delete the Backgrounds zipped folder.
4. Close the Pictures library window.

To Sign Out of Your Account and Turn Off the Computer

After completing your work with Windows, you should follow these steps to end your session by signing out of your account and then turning off the computer.

1. Display the Charms bar.
2. Tap or click the Settings charm.
3. Tap or click the Power button to display the Power menu.
4. Tap or click the Shut down button to sign out of your account and shut down the computer.

Chapter Summary

In this chapter, you have learned about the Computer folder window. You learned how to view the properties of drives and folders, as well as how to view their content. You worked with files and folders in the Pictures library, reviewed and changed their properties, and viewed images in the Photos app and as a slide show. As part of this process, you also learned how to copy and move files as well as how to create folders. Finally, you gained knowledge of how to zip folders so that you can share them. The items listed below include all of the new Windows skills you have learned in this chapter.

1. Open and Maximize the Computer Folder Window (WIN 51)
2. Display Properties for the Local Disk (C:) Drive in the Details Pane (WIN 52)
3. Display the Local Disk (C:) Properties Dialog Box (WIN 53)
4. Close the Local Disk (C:) Properties Dialog Box (WIN 54)
5. Switch Folders Using the Address Bar (WIN 55)
6. View the Contents of a Drive (WIN 56)
7. Preview the Properties of a Folder (WIN 57)
8. Display Properties for the Windows Folder in the Details Pane (WIN 57)
9. Display All of the Properties of the Windows Folder (WIN 58)
10. View the Contents of a Folder (WIN 59)
11. Search for a File and Folder in a Folder Window (WIN 60)
12. Clear the Search Box (WIN 61)
13. Use Shake to Minimize and Restore All Windows (WIN 62)
14. Use Snap to Maximize Windows (WIN 63)
15. Use the Show Desktop Button to Minimize All Windows (WIN 63)
16. Restore a Window (WIN 64)
17. Search for Pictures (WIN 66)
18. Copy Files to the Pictures Library (WIN 67)
19. Create a Folder in the Pictures Library (WIN 69)
20. Move Multiple Files into a Folder (WIN 71)
21. Refresh the Image on a Folder (WIN 72)
22. View and Change the Properties of a Picture (WIN 72)
23. View a Picture in the Photos App (WIN 75)
24. View Pictures as a Slide Show (WIN 76)
25. End a Slide Show (WIN 77)
26. Zip a Folder (WIN 78)
27. View the Contents of a Zipped Folder (WIN 79)

Apply Your Knowledge

Use Windows 8 and its apps to perform the following tasks.

File and App Properties

Instructions: You want to demonstrate to a friend how to display the properties of an image, display the image using the Paint app instead of the Windows Photo Viewer app, and print the image. You also want to demonstrate how to display the properties of an app.

Part 1: Displaying File Properties
1. Display the desktop and then tap or click the File Explorer app button to open the File Explorer window.
2. Tap or click the Computer icon in the navigation pane to display its contents.
3. Double-tap or double-click the Local Disk (C:) icon.
4. Double-tap or double-click the Windows folder.
5. Search for the img3 picture file. If the img3 file is not available on your computer, find another image file.
6. Press and hold, then release, or right-click the img3 icon. Tap or click Properties on the shortcut menu. Answer the following questions about the img3 file:
   a. What type of file is img3?
   b. What app is used to open the img3 image?
   c. What is the path for the location of the img3 file?
   d. What is the size (in bytes) of the img3 file?
   e. When was the file created?
   f. When was the file last modified?
   g. When was the file last accessed?

Part 2: Using the Paint App to Display an Image
1. Tap or click the Change button in the img3 Properties dialog box. Answer the following question:
   a. Which app(s) can you use to open the file?
2. Tap or click the Paint icon in the dialog box.
3. Tap or click the OK button in the img3 Properties dialog box.
4. Double-tap or double-click the img3 icon to run the Paint app and open the img3 file in the img3 – Paint window (Figure 2–47 on the next page).
5. Print the image by tapping or clicking the File tab on the ribbon, tapping or clicking the Print command, and then tapping or clicking the Print button (Print dialog box).
6. Close the Paint window. Do not save any changes.

Part 3: Resetting the App Selection
1. Press and hold, then release, or right-click the img3 icon. Tap or click Properties on the shortcut menu.
2. Tap or click the Change button (img3 Properties dialog box).
3. If necessary, tap or click the Windows Photo Viewer icon in the dialog box to select the icon.
4. Tap or click the OK button.

Continued >

Apply Your Knowledge *continued*

Figure 2–47

Part 4: Displaying App Properties
1. Return to the search results in the Windows folder and clear the Search box.
2. Scroll through the file list until the HelpPane icon appears. If the HelpPane icon does not appear, scroll to display another file.
3. Press and hold, then release, or right-click the icon. Tap or click Properties on the shortcut menu. Answer the following questions:
   a. What type of file is selected?
   b. What is the file's description?
   c. What is the path of the file?
   d. What size is the file when stored on disk?
4. Tap or click the Cancel button (HelpPane.exe Properties dialog box).
5. Close the Windows window.

Extend Your Knowledge

Extend the skills you learned in this chapter and experiment with new skills. You might need to use Help to complete the assignment.

Creating a Picture

Instructions: You want to use Paint to design a get well soon greeting for a friend and then print the message. Because you do not know the location of the Paint app, you first will search to find it.

Part 1: Searching for the Paint App
1. Display the Charms bar and then tap or click the Search charm.
2. Type `paint` in the Search box.
3. Tap or click Paint to run the Paint app (Figure 2–48).

Part 2: Creating a Bitmap Image

1. Use the Pencil button shown in Figure 2–48 to write the message, Get Well Soon! *Hint:* Hold down the left mouse button to write and release the left mouse button to stop writing. If you make a mistake and want to start over, tap or click the Undo button on the Quick Access Toolbar.
2. Tap or click the File tab on the ribbon and then tap or click Save as. When the Save As dialog box is displayed, type `Get Well Soon` in the File name text box, if necessary tap or click the Pictures library in the navigation pane, and then tap or click the Save button (Save As dialog box) to save the file in the Pictures library.
3. Exit Paint.

Figure 2–48

Part 3: Viewing and Printing the Get Well Soon Image

1. Open the Pictures library folder.
2. Double-tap or double-click the Get Well Soon icon in the Pictures window to open the picture in the Photos app.
3. After viewing the image in the Photos app, display the desktop.
4. Display the Share tab, and then tap or click Print (Share tab | Send group) to display the Print Pictures dialog box.
5. Tap or click the Print button (Print Pictures dialog box) to print the image.
6. Close the Print Pictures dialog box.

Part 4: Deleting the Get Well Soon Image

1. Tap or click the Get Well Soon icon to select the file.
2. Tap or click the Delete button (Home tab | Organize group).
3. Close the Pictures library window.

In the Lab

Use the guidelines, concepts, and skills presented in this chapter to increase your knowledge of Windows 8. Labs are listed in order of increasing difficulty.

Lab 1: Using Search to Find Picture Files

Instructions: You know that searching is an important feature of Windows. You decide to use the Search box to find the images on the hard disk. You will store the files in a folder in the Pictures library and then print the images.

Part 1: Searching for Files in the Search Results Window
1. If necessary, start Windows and sign in to your account.
2. Display the desktop.
3. Tap or click the File Explorer app button. Navigate to the Computer folder. Maximize the Computer folder window.
4. Double-tap or double-click Local Disk (C:), and then double-tap or double-click the Windows folder to open it.
5. In the Search box, type `bears` as the entry.
6. Copy the image to the Pictures library using the navigation pane.

Part 2: Searching for Groups of Files
1. Navigate to the Computer folder. Maximize the Computer folder window.
2. Double-tap or double-click Local Disk (C:) and then double-tap or double-click the Windows folder to open it.
3. In the Search box of the Windows folder, type `img1*` as the search text (Figure 2–49).
4. Answer the following question:
   a. How many files were found?
5. Tap or click the img101 icon to select the icon. If the img101 icon does not appear, select another icon.
6. Copy the image to the Pictures library.

Figure 2–49

Part 3: Creating the More Backgrounds Folder in the Pictures Library

1. If necessary, navigate to the Pictures library. Tap or click the New folder button on the Quick Access Toolbar, type More Backgrounds in the new folder's text box, and then press the ENTER key.
2. Select the icons of the images you copied to the Pictures library and then move the images to the More Backgrounds folder.
3. Press and hold, then release, or right-click an open area of the window and refresh the image on the More Backgrounds folder.

Part 4: Printing the Images

1. Open the More Backgrounds folder.
2. Select the pictures.
3. Display the Share tab, tap or click the Print button (Share tab | Send group) and then tap or click the Print button (Print Pictures dialog box) to print the photos.
4. Delete the Backgrounds folder from the Pictures library.
5. Close the Pictures library window.

In the Lab

Lab 2: Finding Pictures Online

Instructions: A friend informs you that the Internet is a great source of photos, pictures, and images. You decide to run Internet Explorer, search for well-known company logos on the Internet, and then save them in a folder. A **logo** is an image that identifies businesses, government agencies, products, and other entities. In addition, you want to print the logos.

Part 1: Running the Internet Explorer App Using the File Explorer

1. Display the desktop and then double-click the File Explorer app button.
2. In the navigation pane, if necessary, click the white arrow next to Computer to display its contents.
3. Tap or click the white arrow next to Local Disk (C:) to display its contents.
4. Tap or click the white arrow next to the Program Files folder to display its contents.
5. Display the contents of the Internet Explorer folder.
6. Double-tap or double-click the iexplore icon to run Internet Explorer and open the Internet Explorer window.

Part 2: Finding and Saving Logo Images

1. Type www.google.com in the address bar in the Internet Explorer window, and then tap or click the Go button.
2. Locate the Google logo icon. Press and hold, then release, or right-click the icon, tap or click 'Save picture as' on the shortcut menu, name the file Google logo, and then tap or click the Save button (Save As dialog box) to save the logo in the Pictures library. If you are unable to save this image, contact your instructor for an alternate image to save for this step.
3. Type www.microsoft.com in the address bar and then tap or click the Go button. Locate the Microsoft picture that matches the one in Figure 2–50 and use the file name, Microsoft logo, to save the Microsoft logo in the Pictures library.
4. Close the Internet Explorer window.

Continued >

In the Lab *continued*

5. Make the File Explorer window the active window and navigate to the Pictures library. The Google logo and Microsoft image appear in the Pictures window (Figure 2–50). The logos in the Pictures library window on your computer might be different from the logos shown in Figure 2–50 if the businesses have changed their logos.

Part 3: Displaying File Properties
1. Press and hold, then release, or right-click each logo file in the Pictures library, tap or click Properties on the shortcut menu, answer the following questions about the logos, and then close the Properties dialog box.
   a. What type of file is the Google logo file?
   b. What type of file is the Microsoft logo file?
2. Tap or click an open area of the Pictures library to deselect the logo file.

Part 4: Creating the Logos Folder in the Pictures Library
1. Create a new folder in the Pictures library, type Logos in the new folder's text box, and then press the ENTER key.
2. Tap or click the item check boxes for each logo to select the files.
3. Drag the icons to the Logos folder.
4. Refresh the image on the Logos folder.

Part 5: Printing the Logo Images
1. Open the Logos folder.
2. Select both of the logos.
3. Display the Share tab, tap or click the Print button (Share tab | Send group), and then tap or click the Print button (Print Pictures dialog box) to print the pictures.
4. Delete the Logos folder from the Pictures library.
5. Close the Pictures window.

Figure 2–50

In the Lab

Lab 3: Managing Your Music

Instructions: You want to investigate the different ways you can organize the music stored on your computer. Once you determine which method of organizing your music you prefer, you decide that you want to add to your music collection. First you will learn about the copyright laws that pertain to digital music and then you will research a few websites that allow you to download music files.

Part 1: Researching Copyright Laws Regarding Digital Music Files

1. Tap or click the Internet Explorer app button on the taskbar. Type `www.copyright.gov` in the address bar and then press the ENTER key. Tap or click the link to display the Frequently Asked Questions, and then answer the following questions:

    a. Can you copyright a domain name?

    b. Can a minor claim a copyright?

    c. What does a copyright protect?

Part 2: Finding Music Online

1. Type `www.globalmusicproject.org` in the address bar, press the ENTER key, and then answer the following questions:

    a. What types of music can be downloaded from this website?

    b. What is the Global Music Project?

    c. Would you use this service?

2. Type `rhapsody.com` in the address bar, press the ENTER key (Figure 2–51), and then answer the following questions:

    a. What does Rhapsody provide?

    b. On what types of devices can you use Rhapsody to listen to music?

    c. Is there a fee for using this service?

    d. Would you use this service?

Figure 2–51

Continued >

In the Lab *continued*

3. Type `www.apple.com/itunes` in the address bar, press the ENTER key, and then answer the following questions:
   a. What is the latest version of iTunes?
   b. What is the iTunes Player?
   c. What is the top song right now on the iTunes Charts?
   d. Would you use this service?

Cases and Places

Apply your creative thinking and problem-solving skills to design and implement a solution.

1: Finding Apps
Academic
You are interested in identifying which apps are installed on your school computer. To find all the apps, you decide to search the Program Files folder on the computer. Using techniques you learned in this chapter, open the Program Files folder on drive C. Search for *.exe files. Summarize your findings in a brief report. Be sure to indicate the number of apps you found.

2: Researching Photo Printing Sites
Personal
Now that you know how to work with the Pictures library, you want to find websites where you can upload and print your photos. Using the Internet, search for three photo printing websites. Find the prices per 4 × 6 photo and which file formats are required, and explore any other photo products that you would be interested in purchasing. Write a brief report that compares the three websites and indicate which one you would use.

3: Researching Data Security
Professional
Data stored on disk is one of a company's most valuable assets. If that data were to be stolen, lost, or compromised so that it could not be accessed, the company could go out of business. Therefore, companies go to great lengths to protect their data. Working with classmates, research how the companies where you each work handle their backups. Find out how each one protects its data against malware, unauthorized access, and even against natural disasters such as fire and floods. Prepare a brief report that describes the companies' procedures. In your report, point out any areas where you find a company has not protected its data adequately.

LEARN ONLINE
Reinforce what you learned in this chapter with games, exercises, training, and many other online activities and resources.

Student Companion Site: Reinforce chapter terms and concepts using review questions, flash cards, practice tests, and interactive learning games, such as a crossword puzzle. These and other online activities and resources are available at no additional cost on www.cengagebrain.com. Visit www.cengage.com/ct/studentdownload for detailed instructions about accessing the resources available at the Student Companion Site.

Microsoft **Windows 8**

3 Personalizing Windows

Objectives

You will have mastered the material in this chapter when you can:

- Differentiate among the various types of user accounts
- Create user accounts
- Understand cloud computing
- Personalize the lock screen
- Customize the Start screen
- Create a picture password
- Turn off a live tile
- Create a tile group on the Start screen
- Name a tile group

3 | Personalizing Windows

Introduction

One of the best ways to improve productivity while using a computer is to personalize your work environment. For example, you can rearrange the tiles on the Start screen so that the tiles you use most often are first or remove tiles for apps you do not use frequently. Similarly, users often personalize their computers by adding unique touches. This includes changing their lock screen and Start screen to display the apps and colors relevant to them. By personalizing the work environment, users feel more in tune with their computers, which can put them more at ease and lead to improved productivity.

Overview

As you read this chapter, you will learn how to personalize your Windows 8 environment by performing these general tasks:

- Add an account
- Customize the lock screen
- Personalize the Start screen
- Manipulate tiles
- Create and name a tile group

User Account

A **user account** is a collection of information that Windows requires about a computer user. When you sign in to an account, the Start screen shows the user account that is signed in at the upper-right corner of the screen. Information is saved for each user account, including the user name, password, picture, and rights and permissions the user has for accessing a computer or network resources. User accounts make it possible for each user to perform tasks, such as sign in to the computer, keep information confidential and computer settings protected, customize Windows, store files in unique folders, and maintain a personal list of favorite websites.

Normally, user accounts operate in standard user mode, which allows you to use most of the capabilities of the computer. A standard user cannot install software that affects other users or change system settings that affect security. An administrator account has full control of the computer and operating system and can change user permissions, install software that affects all users, and change all system settings. When a task requires administrator access, depending on how Windows is configured, the User Account Control feature might prompt you to authorize the task. By default, you are asked for permission only when programs attempt to make a change to the computer. Once authorized, the user has temporary administrator privileges. After the task is finished, the user returns to standard user mode. User Account Control is designed to prevent malicious software from being installed inadvertently, even by administrators. For standard user accounts, the user needs to know an administrator account user name and the password to authorize User Account Control. Only administrators are prompted to continue without requiring a user name and password. Table 3–1 provides a list of the different privileges for the account types.

Table 3–1 User Accounts and Privileges	
User Account Type	Privileges
Administrator	• Create, change, and delete user accounts and groups
	• Install programs
	• Set folder sharing
	• Set permissions
	• Access all files
	• Take ownership of files
	• Grant rights to other user accounts and to themselves
	• Install or remove hardware devices
	• Sign in using safe mode
Standard	• Change the password and picture for their own user accounts
	• Use programs that have been installed on the computer
	• View permissions
	• Create, change, and delete files in their libraries
	• View files in shared document folders
Guest	• Same as standard account, but cannot create a password
	• Is turned off by default, and must be turned on before it can be used

What Is a Local Account?

Windows supports Microsoft accounts and local accounts. A **local account** is an account that works on only one computer. A local account can be either an administrative or a standard account. A local account does not integrate automatically with the cloud, which enables features such as saving files on SkyDrive. **SkyDrive** is a cloud storage location used for storing files on the Internet and for sharing files with other users.

What Is a Microsoft Account?

If you create a Microsoft account on Microsoft's website, you can have access to email, SkyDrive, and Microsoft Office web apps. When you are signed in with a Microsoft account, you can access the services provided on the web for Microsoft account holders. Apps that support Microsoft accounts will allow you to use the associated services that a local account may not be able to use, such as SkyDrive. When you add a Microsoft account to your computer, like a local account, it can be an administrative or a standard account.

When using a Microsoft account, your sign-in settings can be saved on the Internet. When you sign in to Windows on another computer, your settings will be used from your Microsoft account. You can sync your account to the web, which allows you to carry your settings from computer to computer without needing a local account. In some lab settings, you may not be able to use your Microsoft account if the lab does not allow you to sign in without a local account. Your instructor can tell you if you can sign in using your Microsoft account.

To Create a Microsoft Account

The following steps create a Microsoft account. *Why? You might want to have a Microsoft account so that you can save files on SkyDrive and synchronize your user settings.*

1
- Click the Desktop tile to display the desktop (Figure 3–1).

Figure 3–1

2
- Tap or click the Internet Explorer app button on the taskbar to run Internet Explorer (Figure 3–2).

Figure 3–2

3

- Type `windows.live.com` in the address bar to display the windows.live.com webpage (Figure 3–3).

Windows live home page

Figure 3–3

4

- Tap or click the 'Sign up now' link to display the Sign up - Microsoft account webpage (Figure 3–4).
- Complete the Microsoft Account form to create your account.
- Tap or click the I accept button at the bottom of the form.
- Tap or click the Close button to exit Internet Explorer.

Figure 3–4

What Is Cloud Computing?

Cloud computing is the use of computing resources (hardware and software) that are delivered as a service over the Internet or any other network to which you may be connected. Primarily, services, apps, settings, and so forth would be stored on the cloud. This allows for greater portability because you can move from computer to computer and use the files you have stored on the cloud. For example, you can save your files from a school computer on the cloud and then go home and access the same files from your home computer.

This provides great flexibility because you do not need to have your account or files stored on each computer you use. Instead, you can work online and store your work online, without needing to use external storage devices to pass information from computer to computer.

Setting Up User Accounts

Windows users who want to allow multiple people use of their computer can add an account for each user. When adding an account, you can add either a local or Microsoft account. For the Microsoft account to be used, the computer should have an Internet connection. Once you have added the accounts, different users then can sign in to their account by selecting it on the sign-in screen.

To add an account, you must change your PC settings. The 'Change PC settings' command can be used to customize your Windows environment. Adding accounts is one of the ways to personalize your computer.

To Add a Local Account

The following steps add a local account for SC Student. *Why? You have decided to let another person use your computer.*

1
- Display the Charms bar.
- Tap or click the Settings charm to display the Settings menu (Figure 3–5).

Figure 3–5

Setting Up User Accounts **WIN 95**

2
- Tap or click 'Change PC settings' to display the PC settings pane (Figure 3–6).

PC settings pane

Figure 3–6

3
- Tap or click Users in the PC settings pane to display the Users settings in the right pane (Figure 3–7).

Q&A Why does my account information look different from the one shown in Figure 3–7?
The information that is displayed depends on your account settings. The account that displays on your computer may be configured differently.

Users command

local account

account settings for current account displayed in right pane

'Add a user' button

Figure 3–7

WIN 96 Windows Chapter 3 Personalizing Windows

4
- Tap or click the 'Add a user' button in the right pane to display the Add a user screen (Figure 3–8).

Figure 3–8

5
- Tap or click the 'Sign in without a Microsoft account' link to display account options (Figure 3–9).

Figure 3–9

Setting Up User Accounts **WIN 97**

6

- Tap or click the Local account button to display the local account form (Figure 3–10).

Figure 3–10

7

- Enter the information for the new account.
- Tap or click the Next button to continue (Figure 3–11).

Figure 3–11

WIN 98   **Windows Chapter 3**   Personalizing Windows

8
- Tap or click the Finish button to add the account.
- Scroll down to display the accounts available on your computer (Figure 3–12).

Figure 3–12

To Add a Microsoft Account

The following steps add a Microsoft account. ***Why?*** *You recently created a Microsoft account and would like to add it so that you can use the cloud storage options associated with a Microsoft account.*

1
- Tap or click the 'Add a user' button in the right pane (shown in Figure 3–12) to display the Add a user screen (Figure 3–13).

Figure 3–13

2
- Type your Microsoft account email address into the Email address text box.
- Tap or click the Next button to continue creating the account (Figure 3–14).
- Tap or click the Finish button to add the account.

Q&A | Why is the email address on my screen different from Figure 3–14?
You used your own Microsoft account. The one in the figure is not your email address.

Figure 3–14

To Sign In to a Microsoft Account

To sign in to a different account, you will first need to sign out of the current account. After you have signed out, you will be able to sign in to the newly created Microsoft account.

1 Display the Charms bar.

2 Tap or click the Start charm on the Charms bar to return to the Start screen.

3 Tap or click the user icon to display user options.

4 Tap or click Sign out to sign out of your account.

5 Swipe or click the lock screen to display the sign-in screen.

6 Tap or click the user icon for your Microsoft account (for SC Series Microsoft, in this case) on the sign-in screen, which depending on settings, either will display a second sign-in screen that contains a password text box or will display the Windows Start screen.

7 If Windows displays a password text box, type your password in the text box and then tap or click the Submit button to sign in to your account and display the Start screen.

Personalizing the Lock and Start Screens

One way to personalize your Windows settings is to change the appearance of the lock screen and the Start screen. For the lock screen, you can change the apps that are displayed to the apps that you want or use most frequently. They will run in the background and be available whenever the lock screen is displayed. You can change the background pattern, as well as the color scheme, displayed on the Start screen.

You personalize the lock screen and Start screen using the PC settings pane.

To Personalize the Lock Screen

The following steps add the Weather app to the lock screen. *Why? You want to be able to check the weather quickly without having to return to the Start screen each time.*

1
- Display the Charms bar.
- Tap or click the Settings charm to display the Settings menu (Figure 3–15).
- Tap or click 'Change PC settings' to display the PC settings pane.

Figure 3–15

2
- Scroll down in the right pane to display the Lock screen apps area (Figure 3–16).

Figure 3–16

3
- Tap or click the first plus sign icon to display the Choose an app menu (Figure 3–17).

Figure 3–17

4

- Tap or click the Weather app to add it to the lock screen apps (Figure 3–18).

Figure 3–18

To Change the Start Screen Color Scheme

Why? *You want to change the color scheme of the Start screen to light blue.* The following steps change the Start screen color scheme.

1

- Tap or click Start screen in the right pane to display the Start screen personalization options (Figure 3–19).

Figure 3–19

2

- Tap or click the light blue color scheme to change the color scheme to light blue (Figure 3–20).

Figure 3–20

To Change the Start Screen Background Pattern

Why? You want a pattern that makes the light blue color stand out. The following step changes the Start screen background pattern.

1

- Tap or click the fourth background pattern in the first row to change the background pattern (Figure 3–21).

Figure 3–21

Adding a Picture Password

Instead of using a password that you have to type in, Windows allows you to use a picture password instead. A **picture password** involves you selecting a picture and then adding gestures to use for your password. A gesture can be a circle, a straight line, or a tap. When you sign in to your account, you will use those gestures to sign in, rather than a password. You always can go back and remove the picture password should you no longer want to use it. Also, you can change your picture password to use a different picture or different gestures.

To Copy a Picture

You will need a picture to use when creating a picture password. The following steps copy img1 from the Windows folder to the Pictures library.

1. Display the desktop.
2. Click the File Explorer app button to run File Explorer.
3. Display the Windows folder.
4. Type `img1.jpg` in the Search box and then press the ENTER key to search for the img1 picture.
5. Tap or click the item check box for the img1 picture to select the file.
6. Tap or click the Copy button (Home tab | Clipboard group) to copy the files to the Clipboard.
7. Tap or click the Pictures folder in the navigation pane to display the Pictures library.
8. Tap or click the Paste button (Home tab | Clipboard group) to paste the file in the Pictures library.
9. Display the PC settings pane.

To Create a Picture Password

Why? You want to use a picture password so that it is easier to enter on a touch-enabled device. Once you create the gestures, you will have to repeat them to make sure you are using the same exact gestures. If you recognize that you have made a mistake, you can tap or click the Start over button to begin again. Should you fail to enter them correctly the second time, you will be prompted to try again. The following steps create a picture password.

Adding a Picture Password **WIN 105**

Windows Chapter 3

❶
- Tap or click Users in the PC settings pane to display user account information in the right pane (Figure 3–22).

Figure 3–22

❷
- Tap or click the 'Create a picture password' button to display the Create a picture password screen (Figure 3–23).

Figure 3–23

3
- Type your password in the Password text box and then tap or click the OK button to display the picture password instructions (Figure 3–24).

Figure 3–24

4
- Tap or click the Choose picture button to display a list of pictures.
- Tap or click the img1 file to select the picture (Figure 3–25).

Figure 3–25

5
- Tap or click the Open button to open the picture (Figure 3–26).

Figure 3–26

6
- Tap or click the 'Use this picture' button to use the picture (Figure 3–27).

Figure 3–27

7
- Perform three gestures to add gestures to the picture password.
- Perform the three gestures again to confirm the picture password.
- Click the Finish button to return to the PC settings pane (Figure 3–28).

Figure 3–28

Is a Picture Password Secure?

Because picture passwords use gestures that you have made, they are just as secure as regular passwords. In fact, some would say they are more secure because they use touch gestures and not letters, numbers, and so on. Someone would have to guess which gestures you used, in what order, and where on the picture you made them to guess your password.

Customizing the Start Screen

In Chapter 1, you moved and resized tiles on the Start screen. Using the App bar, you also can display all apps, unpin apps from the Start screen, and turn live tiles off and on. Unpinning an app does not uninstall it; rather, it just removes the tile from the Start screen.

You also can change the tile layout on the Start screen. Changing the layout allows you to organize your tiles in the order that works best for you. You can create new tile groups to help in the organization. A **tile group** is a collection of tiles in one section of the Start screen.

After you have created the tile group, you can move other tiles by dragging the tiles to that group. After you have created your tile groups, you can use **Semantic Zoom**, which is a button on the Start screen that allows you to zoom out to view your tiles. You also can zoom with touch gestures or your mouse. Once zoomed out, you can give a name to the new tile group. Once named, the tile group name will be displayed on the Start screen.

To Display All Apps

Using the App bar, you can display all the apps on your computer. The following steps display all apps. *Why? You want to see which apps are installed on your computer.*

1
- Press the WINDOWS key to return to the Start screen.
- Swipe from the bottom of the Start screen or right-click an open space on the Start screen to display the App bar (Figure 3–29).

Figure 3–29

2
- Tap or click the All apps button to display the list of the installed apps (Figure 3–30).

Figure 3–30

To Run an App from the Apps List

The following steps display the Weather app. *Why? You want to see if clicking an app in the Apps list runs the app the same way it does when run from the Start screen.*

1
- Tap or click the Weather app to run the Weather app (Figure 3–31).

2
- Display the Charms bar.
- Tap or click the Start charm to return to the Start screen.

Figure 3–31

To Pin an App to the Start Screen

When an app that you regularly use is not on the Start screen, you can pin it to place it there. *Why? The app then can be easily accessed on the Start screen, eliminating the need to search for it.* The following steps pin the Reader app to the Start screen.

Customizing the Start Screen **WIN 111**

❶
- Swipe from the bottom of the Start screen or right-click an open space on the Start screen to display the App bar (Figure 3–32).

Figure 3–32

❷
- Tap or click the All apps button to display the Apps list (Figure 3–33).

Figure 3–33

3

- Press and hold or right-click the Reader app to select it and display the App bar (Figure 3–34).

Figure 3–34

4

- Tap or click the 'Pin to Start' button to pin the app to the Start screen.
- Display the Start screen.
- Scroll to the right to display the newly pinned Reader app (Figure 3–35).

Figure 3–35

Customizing the Start Screen **WIN 113**

To Unpin an App from the Start Screen

Why? *You discovered that you no longer use an app very often and want to remove it from the Start screen to save space.* When you no longer want an app to appear on the Start screen, you can unpin the app. The following steps unpin the Sports app from the Start screen.

1
- Scroll to the left to display the Sports tile (Figure 3–36).

Figure 3–36

2
- Press and hold or right-click the tile to select it and display the App bar (Figure 3–37).

Figure 3–37

3

- Click the 'Unpin from Start' button to unpin the tile from the Start screen (Figure 3–38).

Figure 3–38

To Turn Off a Live Tile

In Chapter 1, you learned that some tiles are live tiles that actively display content. If you would rather not have them display the live content, you can turn off the live tile. *Why? You may decide that you want the tile to show a logo instead of active content.*

The following steps turn off the Travel live tile.

1

- Press and hold or right-click the Travel tile to select it and display the App bar (Figure 3–39).

Figure 3–39

2
- Tap or click the 'Turn live tile off' button to turn off the live tile (Figure 3–40).

Figure 3–40

Managing Tile Layout

Along with the other personalization you have done, you can manipulate the tile layout on the Start screen. In Chapter 1, you learned how to move a tile. Now you will learn how to create tile groups, name tile groups, and place tiles into groups. As discussed earlier, a tile group is a collection of tiles. The Start screen already contains several groups. For example, the Desktop tile is in the first tile group.

Creating a new tile group is accomplished by dragging a tile to the right or left until the new group is created. Once created, you can zoom out or in so that you can reorder and name your tile groups. This allows you to place the tile group you use most often on the left side of the Start screen to reduce scrolling. By naming a tile group, you can identify what the tiles are used for in that tile group.

To Zoom to View Tile Groups

Why? *You want to see the tile groups at the same time without scrolling.* The following steps zoom out and then zoom in to view tile groups.

1

- Stretch, or press the CTRL key and scroll backward with the mouse wheel to zoom out (Figure 3–41).

tile groups zoomed out

Figure 3–41

2

- Pinch, or press the CTRL key and scroll forward using the mouse wheel to zoom in (Figure 3–42).

tile groups returned to normal size

Figure 3–42

Other Ways

1. Press CTRL+PLUS SIGN (+); press CTRL+MINUS SIGN (–)

Managing Tile Layout **WIN 117**

To Create a New Tile Group

The following steps create a new group using the People tile. *Why? You want to place tiles for apps you frequently use together so that they are next to each other. Organizing your tiles logically and in groups can make it much easier to locate them.*

1
- Drag the People tile to the left until a vertical bar appears to create a new tile group (Figure 3–43).

Figure 3–43

2
- Release the People tile to create the new tile group (Figure 3–44).

Figure 3–44

To Move a Tile to a Different Tile Group

The following step moves the Photos tile to the same tile group as the People tile. *Why? You have decided that you would also like to put the Photos tile in the new tile group because you often use that app when you use the People app.*

1
- Drag the Photos tile below the People tile.
- Release the Photos tile to add it to the tile group (Figure 3–45).

Figure 3–45

To Reorder Tile Groups

The following steps move the second group to the right. *Why? When you use a group more often, you can move it to the left to make it accessible without scrolling. Conversely, if you use a group less often, you can move it to the right.*

1
- Pinch, or press the CTRL key and scroll backward using the mouse wheel to zoom out (Figure 3–46).

Figure 3–46

2

- Drag the second group to the right so that it follows the third group to switch the two groups (Figure 3–47).

Figure 3–47

To Name a Tile Group

Why? *You want to personalize your Start screen by naming your groups so that you know which tiles should be placed in that group.* After you name your tile group, you can remove the name by repeating these steps, but deleting the text from the 'Name this group of tiles' text box.

The following steps name a tile group.

1

- Press and hold or right-click the first tile group to display the App bar (Figure 3–48).

Figure 3–48

2
- Tap or click the Name group button on the App bar to display a dialog box (Figure 3–49).

Figure 3–49

3
- Type Favorites in the 'Name this group of tiles' text box to enter a name for the tile group (Figure 3–50).

Figure 3–50

Managing Tile Layout **WIN 121**

4
- Tap or click the Name button in the dialog box to name the tile group (Figure 3–51).

Q&A How can I remove the name from a tile group?
To remove the name from a tile group, repeat Steps 1 through 4. Instead of typing a name for the tile group in Step 3, delete all text from the text box.

Figure 3–51

5
- Pinch, or press the CTRL key and scroll forward using the mouse wheel to zoom in (Figure 3–52).

Figure 3–52

To Sign Out of an Account and Shut Down the Computer

The following steps sign out of open accounts and shut down the computer.

1 Display the Charms bar.

2 Tap or click the Start charm on the Charms bar to return to the Start screen.

3 Tap or click the user icon to display user options.

4 Tap or click Sign out to sign out of Windows.

5 Display the Charms bar.

6 Tap or click the Settings charm on the Charms bar to display the Settings menu.

7 Tap or click the Power button to display the Power menu.

8 Tap or click Shut down to sign out of your account and shut down the computer.

Chapter Summary

In this chapter, you learned how to personalize your Windows Start screen. You created user accounts, learned about cloud storage, and signed in using a Microsoft account. You customized the lock screen, changed the design of the Start screen, and created a picture password. You also learned how to arrange tiles on the Start screen by creating and naming new tile groups. Finally, you rearranged the tile groups for easier access to the tiles you use the most. The items listed below include all of the new Windows skills you have learned in this chapter.

1. Create a Microsoft Account (WIN 92)
2. Add a Local Account (WIN 94)
3. Add a Microsoft Account (WIN 98)
4. Personalize the Lock Screen (WIN 100)
5. Change the Start Screen Color Scheme (WIN 102)
6. Change the Start Screen Background Pattern (WIN 103)
7. Create a Picture Password (WIN 104)
8. Display All Apps (WIN 109)
9. Run an App from the Apps List (WIN 110)
10. Pin an App to the Start Screen (WIN 110)
11. Unpin an App from the Start Screen (WIN 113)
12. Turn Off a Live Tile (WIN 114)
13. Zoom to View Tile Groups (WIN 115)
14. Create a New Tile Group (WIN 117)
15. Move a Tile to a Different Tile Group (WIN 118)
16. Reorder Tile Groups (WIN 118)
17. Name a Tile Group (WIN 119)

Apply Your Knowledge

Changing the Start Screen

Instructions: You want to customize the look and design of the Start screen by changing theme colors and backgrounds, moving tiles, and naming tile groups.

Part 1: Changing the Start Screen Color Scheme and Background
1. Display the Charms bar and then tap or click the Settings charm to display the Settings menu.
2. Click Personalization in the PC settings pane to display the personalization options in the right pane.
3. Tap or click 'Change PC settings' to display the PC settings pane (Figure 3–53).
4. Tap or click Start screen in the right pane to display the Start screen personalization options.
5. Tap or click the fourth background option in the second row to change the Start screen background.
6. Tap or click the yellow color scheme to change the Start screen color scheme to yellow.

Part 2: Creating Tile Groups
1. Switch to the Start screen.
2. Drag the Messaging tile to the left to create a new tile group.
3. Drag the Mail tile to the newly created tile group.
4. Stretch, or press the CTRL key and scroll backward using the mouse wheel to zoom out.
5. Press and hold or right-click the newly created tile group to select it and display the App bar.
6. Tap or click the Name group button to display a dialog box.
7. Type `Communication` in the 'Name this group of tiles' text box.
8. Click the Name button to assign the tile group name.
9. Stretch, or press the CTRL key and scroll forward using the mouse wheel to zoom in.

Figure 3–53

Extend Your Knowledge

Extend the skills you learned in this chapter and experiment with new skills. You might need to use Help to complete the assignment.

Using Help

Instructions: Use Windows Help and Support to perform the following tasks.

1. Find Help about customizing the Desktop by typing `themes` in the Search text box and then clicking the Search button (Figure 3–54). Tap or click the result titled 'Get started with themes' and then answer the following questions:
   a. What is a desktop background?
   b. What is a screen saver?
   c. What is a window border color?

Figure 3–54

2. Use Windows Help and Support to answer the following questions:
   a. What are My Themes?
   b. What are Windows Default Themes?
   c. What are Basic and High Contrast Themes?

3. Use the Search text box in Windows Help and Support to answer the following questions:
   a. How do you create a theme?
   b. How do you save a theme?
   c. How do you share a theme?
   d. How do you delete a theme?
   e. How do you get more information about the pictures that are included in a particular theme?

4. Close the Windows Help and Support window.

In the Lab

Use the guidelines, concepts, and skills presented in this chapter to increase your knowledge of Windows 8. Labs are listed in order of increasing difficulty.

Lab 1: Customizing Settings

Problem: You would like to customize your lock screen and add a picture password for your user account.

Instructions: Use the PC settings pane to perform the following tasks.

1. Copy the img3 picture from the Windows folder to the Pictures library. You will be using this picture as a picture password later in this exercise.
2. Display the PC settings pane.
3. Click Personalize in the PC settings pane to perform the following tasks:
   a. Tap or click Lock screen in the right pane to display personalization options.
   b. If necessary, scroll to display the Lock screen apps area.
   c. Tap or click one of the add buttons to add a lock screen app.
   d. Tap or click the Weather app on the Choose an app menu to add it to the lock screen.
   e. Tap or click the Calendar icon and then click the 'Don't show quick status here' link to remove it from the lock screen.
4. Click Users in the PC settings pane and then perform the following tasks:
   a. Tap or click the 'Create picture password' button to create a picture password.
   b. After entering your password, tap or click to select the img3 picture that will be used as a picture password (Figure 3–55).
   c. Gesture or use the mouse to add a circle, line, and tap to create a picture password.

Figure 3–55

In the Lab

Lab 2: Creating and Adding an Account

Instructions: You want to add a local account for your friend, Betty Lou. Perform the following steps first to add and then to sign in to a local account.

Part 1: Creating the Local Account
1. Display the PC settings pane and then tap or click Users to display your account information.
2. Tap or click the 'Add a user' button in the right pane to add a user.
3. Tap or click the 'Sign in without a Microsoft account' link to display the account options.
4. Tap or click Local account to create a local account (Figure 3–56).
5. Enter Betty Lou's name, a password, and a hint of your choosing.
6. Follow the remaining steps on the screen to create the account.

Part 2: Switching Accounts
1. Display the Start screen.
2. Tap or click your user icon.
3. Tap or click the Betty Lou icon.
4. Enter the password for Betty Lou to switch to that account.

Part 3: Signing Out of an Account
1. Tap or click the user icon on the Start screen.
2. Tap or click Sign out to sign out of the account.

Figure 3–56

In the Lab

Lab 3: Creating a Microsoft Account

Instructions: Perform the following steps to create a Microsoft account.

Part 1: Creating a Microsoft Account
1. If necessary, connect to the Internet and display the desktop.
2. Click the Internet Explorer app button to run Internet Explorer.
3. Click the web address in the address bar to select it.
4. Type `windows.live.com` in the address bar and then press the ENTER key (Figure 3–57).
5. Tap or click the 'Sign up now' link to create a Microsoft account.
6. Enter your information to create the Microsoft account.

Part 2: Adding a Microsoft Account
1. Display the PC settings pane and then tap or click Users to display your account info in the right pane.
2. Tap or click the 'Add a user' button to add a user.
3. Enter your email address.
4. Tap or click the Next button and then tap or click the Finish button to add the account.

Part 3: Signing Out of an Account
1. Tap or click the user icon on the sign-in screen.
2. Tap or click Sign out to sign out of the account.

Figure 3–57

Cases and Places

Apply your creative thinking and problem-solving skills to design and implement a solution.

1: Assessing Windows 8 Compatibility
Academic
Colors, patterns, and the arrangement of the workplace can have a significant effect on worker productivity. These factors might draw attention to some objects, de-emphasize others, speed the completion of tasks, or even promote desirable moods and attitudes. Working with classmates, visit the Internet, a library, or other research facility to discover how colors, patterns, and arrangements can impact a work environment. Using what you have learned, together with the concepts and techniques presented in this chapter, create the Windows Start screen that you think would help your classmates be more efficient. Write a report describing your Start screen and explaining why you feel it would enhance productivity.

2: Creating a Picture Password
Personal
You recently bought a touch screen computer and want to use a family photo to add a picture password to your account. Download a family photo of your choice to the Pictures library. Add a picture password using the PC Settings pane. Use any three gestures to create the picture password. Write a report describing why you selected the picture you did and which gestures you decided to use. Include any thoughts on the difficulty of others to guess the password.

3: Researching Account Privileges
Professional
You are working in the technical support company for a corporation. Your boss has been wondering if he should allow users to have administrative or standard account privileges. He wants you to research this using Windows Help and Support and the Internet and create a summary for him to use in making his decision. Describe the account types and then list some of the advantages and disadvantages of each. Finally, tell which accounts you would create and explain why.

LEARN ONLINE
Reinforce what you learned in this chapter with games, exercises, training, and many other online activities and resources.

Student Companion Site: Reinforce chapter terms and concepts using review questions, flash cards, practice tests, and interactive learning games, such as a crossword puzzle. These and other online activities and resources are available at no additional cost on www.cengagebrain.com. Visit www.cengagebrain.com/ct/studentdownload for detailed instructions about accessing the resources available at the Student Companion Site.

Appendix A
Creating a Microsoft Account

Introduction

A **Microsoft account** is a free service that provides a personalized Windows experience across devices, apps, and services. If you previously created a Windows Live ID, this now is referred to as your Microsoft account. A Microsoft account consists of an email address and password that you can use to sign in to Windows 8 to connect to the cloud. You can sign in to any Windows 8 computer or mobile device with a Microsoft account to access your apps and customized user settings. These user settings include your lock screen picture, desktop tile layout, apps, spell check dictionaries, Internet Explorer favorites, and accessibility settings. The personalized settings associated with your Windows account are stored on the cloud. As these settings are changed or updated, they are kept in sync with each device you use.

In addition, the Microsoft account allows you to share your photos, documents, apps, and other files from places like SkyDrive, Facebook, and Flickr within Windows. For example, the People app in Windows connects to your Microsoft account to bring your contacts to one convenient location that roams across your Windows computers and phone. Using your Microsoft account credentials, you can connect to your Microsoft account by visiting outlook.com, which provides access to your documents, presentations, spreadsheets, databases, videos, and photos.

To Create a Microsoft Account

You can sign in to a Windows computer with a local user account or a Microsoft account. You can create a new Microsoft account from within Windows or on the web at outlook.com. The following steps create a Microsoft account within Windows after signing in to a user account.

APP 2 Appendix A Creating a Microsoft Account

❶
- Swipe from the right or point to the upper-right corner of the screen to display the Charms bar (Figure A–1).

Figure A–1

❷
- Tap or click the Settings charm on the Charms bar to display the Settings menu (Figure A–2).

Figure A–2

Introduction **APP 3**

3
- Tap or click the 'Change PC settings' command on the Settings menu to display the PC settings pane (Figure A–3).

Figure A–3

4
- Tap or click the Users command in the PC settings pane to display Users options in the right pane.
- If necessary, scroll down to view the 'Add a user' button (Figure A–4).

Figure A–4

Appendix A Creating a Microsoft Account

5
- Tap or click the 'Add a user' button to display the 'Add a user' screen (Figure A–5).

Figure A–5

6
- Tap or click the 'Sign up for a new email address' link to display the 'Sign up for a new email address' screen (Figure A–6).

Figure A–6

7

- Tap or click the Email address text box in the 'Sign up for a new email address' screen, type your desired email address, and then tap or click the arrow to display mail options.
- Tap or click live.com or outlook.com.
- Tap or click the New password text box and type your desired password.
- Tap or click the Reenter password text box and reenter the same password as the previous step.
- Tap or click the First name text box and type your first name.
- Tap or click the Last name text box and type your last name.
- If necessary, tap or click the Country/region of your country of residence.
- Tap or click the ZIP code text box and then type your ZIP code.
- Tap or click the Next button to display the 'Add security info' screen (Figure A–7).

Figure A–7

8

- If necessary, select the Phone number in the 'Add security info' screen and then tap or click your country of residence.
- Tap or click the second Phone number text box and then type your phone number.
- Tap or click the Alternate email text box and then type an alternate email address.
- Tap or click the Secret question arrow and then tap or click the secret question of your choice.
- Tap or click the Answer text box and then type the answer to your secret question.
- Tap or click the Next button to display the Finish up screen (Figure A–8).

Figure A–8

9

- Tap or click the arrows to display and then select the birth date month, day, and year on the Finish up screen.
- Tap or click the appropriate Gender option button to select your gender.
- Tap or click the Next button to agree to the Microsoft services agreement & privacy and cookies statement (Figure A–9).

Figure A–9

10
- Enter the requested characters to confirm and complete your account creation process.
- Tap or click the Next button to create a user account that can sign in to this computer.
- Tap or click the Finish button to add the new user account to your computer.

Other Ways

1. Visit outlook.com, tap or click 'Sign up now' button, fill in your personal information

Appendix B
Windows 8 Security

Introduction

Windows 8 includes strong improvements in performance, security, malware protection, and system reliability. In addition, a number of updated security features help you accomplish three important goals: to enjoy a computer free from malware, including viruses, worms, spyware, and other potentially unwanted software; to have a safer online experience using Windows 8 apps and Web sites; and to understand when a computer is vulnerable and how to protect it from external threats.

Malware, short for malicious software, is a computer program that acts without a user's knowledge and deliberately alters a computer's operations. Examples of malware include viruses, worms, and spyware. A **virus** is a program that attaches itself to another program or file so that it can spread from computer to computer, infecting programs and files as it spreads. Viruses can damage computer software, computer hardware, and files. A computer **worm** copies itself from one computer to another by taking advantage of the features that transport data and information between computers. A worm is dangerous because it has the capability of traveling without being detected and to replicate itself in great volume. For example, if a worm copies itself to every contact in your email address book and then the worm copies itself to the names of all the email addresses of each of your contacts' computers, the effect could result in increased Internet traffic that slows down business networks and the Internet. **Spyware** is a program that is installed on your computer without your consent that monitors the activity that takes place to gather personal information and send it secretly to its creator. Spyware also can be designed to take control of the infected computer.

A **hacker** is an individual who uses his or her expertise to gain unauthorized access to a computer with the intention of learning more about the computer or examining the contents of the computer without the owner's permission.

To Display the Windows Action Center

The Action Center is a central location to view notifications and manage your computer's security by monitoring the status of several essential security features on your computer, including firewall settings, automatic updating, virus protection, spyware and unwanted software protection, Internet security settings, user account control settings, and network access protection. The following steps display the Action Center.

1
- Tap or click the Desktop tile to run the Desktop app.
- Point to the upper-right corner of the desktop to display the Charms bar (Figure B–1).

Figure B–1

2
- Tap or click the Settings charm to display the Settings menu (Figure B–2).

Figure B–2

Introduction **APP 11**

❸
- Tap or click Control Panel on the Settings menu to open the Control Panel window (Figure B–3).

Figure B–3

❹
- Tap or click the 'System and Security' link to open the System and Security window (Figure B–4).

Figure B–4

APP 12   Appendix B   Windows 8 Security

5
- Tap or click the Action Center link in the System and Security window to open the Action Center window (Figure B–5).

Figure B–5

6
- Tap or click the Security section arrow to expand the Security section (Figure B–6).

Figure B–6

Understanding the Action Center

The right pane, which has two expandable sections, displays options to let you review messages and resolve problems. The first section is the Security section. Tapping or clicking the section arrow to the right of the Security heading expands the section and displays security features. Settings labeled On and OK mean that the security feature is turned on and working properly. Settings labeled Off mean that the security feature is turned off and you should turn it on, if appropriate according to that feature. For features that have settings you can change, you will see options for adjusting them. Important messages about security and maintenance settings that need your attention are displayed in the Action Center if an issue arises. Items marked with a preceding red block indicate urgent issues that should be addressed as soon as possible, while items marked in yellow are issues that are not pressing but that you should consider addressing soon.

The second section is the Maintenance section, which allows you to view maintenance features. Similar to the Security section, settings labeled On and OK mean that the maintenance feature is turned on and working, and settings labeled Off mean that the feature is turned off and you should turn it on, if appropriate according to that particular feature. Not all maintenance features have the same options. For example, if Automatic Maintenance is turned on, you will see only the message, No action needed. For some of the features, you also can choose whether or not you want to monitor the messages that pop up when an issue arises. If you choose not to monitor a feature, the status will be listed as, Currently not monitored. As with the security features, if you can change settings, you will see options for adjusting them.

In the left pane of the Action Center window are links to Control Panel Home, Change Action Center settings, Change User Account Control settings, Change Windows SmartScreen settings, View archived messages, and View performance information. **Windows SmartScreen** helps protect your computer by warning you if a downloaded app or file is known to be malware or has an unknown reputation.

Managing Windows Firewall

Windows Firewall is a program that protects your computer from unauthorized users by monitoring and restricting data that travels between your computer and a network or the Internet. Windows Firewall also helps to block, but does not always prevent, computer viruses and worms from infecting your computer. Windows Firewall automatically is turned on when Windows 8 is started. It is recommended that Windows Firewall remain on, unless you have another firewall program actively protecting your computer. **Windows Defender** is an antivirus and malware protection program that is included in Windows 8; you also can install third-party software to protect against viruses and malware.

To Open the Windows Firewall Window

From the Windows Firewall window's right pane, you can monitor and manage the firewall settings for any network to which you are connected. Connected networks normally are classified as home, work, and public networks. Home and work networks are considered private networks and have settings that are different from public networks, which are not considered to be as secure.

From the left pane, you can allow programs or features through Windows Firewall, change notification settings, turn off Windows Firewall, restore default settings, adjust advanced settings, and troubleshoot your network. Windows Firewall is set up with the most secure settings by default, according to Microsoft. The following step opens the Windows Firewall window.

1
- Tap or click the Back button (shown in Figure B–6) in the Action Center window to return to the System and Security window.
- Tap or click the Windows Firewall link to open the Windows Firewall window (Figure B–7).

Q&A Why does my window show a different network?
You can connect to different types of networks. The type of network connection you have will determine whether a home or a public network is displayed.

Figure B–7

To Allow a Feature through the Firewall

You can adjust Windows Firewall settings as needed. For example, if you have an app or feature that you want to allow to communicate through the firewall, you can allow it using the 'Allow an app or feature through Windows Firewall' link. Caution should be used because each app or feature allowed through the firewall carries the risk of making your computer less secure; that is, the computer becomes easier to access and more vulnerable to attacks by hackers. The more apps and features you allow, the more vulnerable the computer. To decrease the risk of security problems, allow only those apps or features that are necessary and recognizable, and promptly remove any app or feature that no longer is required.

One feature that sometimes is allowed for home and work private networks is File and Printer Sharing. This feature allows other computers access to files and printers that you choose to share with the network. The following steps allow File and Printer Sharing through the firewall for private networks only.

❶
- Tap or click the 'Allow an app or feature through Windows Firewall' link to open the Allowed apps window (Figure B–8).

Figure B–8

❷
- Tap or click the Change settings button to enable the 'Allowed apps and features' area.
- If necessary, scroll to display the 'File and Printer Sharing' feature in the 'Allowed apps and features' area (Figure B–9).

Figure B–9

APP 16 Appendix B Windows 8 Security

❸
- Tap or click to select the Private check box for 'File and Printer Sharing' (Figure B–10).

Figure B–10

❹
- Tap or click the OK button to accept the changes and return to the Windows Firewall window (Figure B–11).

Figure B–11

To Disallow a Feature through the Firewall

If you later decide that you do not want to allow a program or feature through the Windows Firewall, you should disallow it. The following steps disallow File and Printer Sharing through the firewall for Private (home/work) networks only.

1
- Tap or click the 'Allow an app or feature through Windows Firewall' link to open the Allowed apps window.
- If necessary, tap or click the Change settings button to access the 'Allowed apps and features' area.
- If necessary, scroll to display the 'File and Print Sharing' feature in the 'Allowed apps and features' list (Figure B–12).

Figure B–12

❷
- Tap or click the Private check box for 'File and Printer Sharing' to remove the check mark (Figure B–13).

Figure B–13

❸
- Tap or click the OK button to accept the changes and return to the Windows Firewall window (Figure B–14).

Figure B–14

Windows Update

Windows Update helps to protect your computer from viruses, worms, and other security risks. When Windows Update is turned on and the computer is connected to the Internet, Windows periodically checks with Microsoft to find updates for your computer and then automatically downloads them. If the Internet connection is lost while downloading an update, Windows resumes downloading when the Internet connection becomes available.

To Install Updates Automatically

You want to make sure that your computer is set to receive critical updates and install them automatically. The following steps configure an automatic update for your Windows Update settings.

1
- Tap or click the 'Up to System and Security' button (shown in Figure B-14) to return to the System and Security window (Figure B-15).

Figure B–15

2
- Tap or click the Windows Update link in the System and Security window to open the Windows Update window (Figure B–16).

APP 20 Appendix B Windows 8 Security

Figure B–16

③
- Tap or click the Change settings link to open the Change settings window (Figure B–17).

④
- If necessary, tap or click 'Install updates automatically (recommended)' in the Important updates list to install important updates to your computer automatically.
- Tap or click the OK button in the Change settings window to save the changes and return to the Windows Update window.
- Close the Windows Update window.

Figure B–17

Protecting against Computer Viruses and Malware

Most computer magazines, daily newspapers, and even television news channels warn of computer virus threats. Although these threats sound alarming, a little common sense and a good antivirus program can ward off even the most malicious viruses.

A computer can be protected against viruses by following these suggestions. First, educate yourself about viruses and how they spread. Downloading a program from the Internet, accessing a website, or receiving an email message can cause a virus to infect your computer. Second, learn the common signs of a virus. Observe any unusual messages that appear on the computer screen, monitor system performance, and watch for missing files and inaccessible hard disks. Third, recognize that programs on removable media might contain viruses, and scan all removable media before copying or opening files.

Windows 8 includes real-time virus detection and protection with Windows Defender. You may decide to install a third-party antivirus program for additional protection or use Windows Defender as your primary virus protection. Windows Defender helps you stay productive by protecting your computer against pop-ups, slow performance, and security threats caused by spyware and other potentially damaging software. When you scan your computer using Windows Defender, it is vital to have the most recent virus definitions. **Definitions** are the files that form a database of all the current virus signatures used by the antivirus software for malware detection. To assist in keeping the definitions up to date, automatically set your Windows Update, which installs new definitions as they are released.

To Scan Using Windows Defender

Windows Defender can notify you when malware attempts to install programs or attempts to change settings on your computer. Windows Defender can be set to scan for malware on a regular basis or at any time on demand. The following steps scan your computer using Windows Defender.

1
- Point to the upper-right corner of the screen to display the Charms bar (Figure B–18).

Figure B–18

2

- Tap or click the Search charm to display the Search menu (Figure B–19).

Figure B–19

3

- Type `defender` as the search text in the in the Search box, and watch the search results appear (Figure B–20).

Figure B–20

Protecting against Computer Viruses and Malware **APP 23**

4
- Tap or click Windows Defender in the search results to open the Windows Defender window (Figure B–21).

Figure B–21

5
- If necessary, tap or click the Quick option button to select it.
- Tap or click the Scan now button to scan your computer for malware (Figure B–22).

Figure B–22

To View the Windows Defender Settings for Automatic Scanning

The following steps display the automatic scanning settings in Windows Defender.

1
- Tap or click the Settings tab in the Windows Defender window (Figure B–23).

2
- If necessary, tap or click the 'Turn on real-time protection (recommended)' check box to select it.
- If necessary, tap or click the Save changes button to save the changes made to the real-time protection settings.
- Close the Windows Defender window.

Figure B–23

Summary

Security is an important issue for computer users. You need to be aware of the possible threats to your computer, as well as the security features that can be used to protect your computer. The Action Center, along with other security features in Windows, allows you to configure the security settings that will help you keep your computer safe.

Index

Note: **Bold** page numbers refer to pages where key terms are defined.

A

accounts. *See also* local accounts; Microsoft accounts; user accounts
  signing out of, WIN 80
Action Center
  displaying, APP 9–12
  panes, APP 13
address bar, switching folders, WIN 55–56
app(s), **WIN 2**, WIN 11–14
  displaying, WIN 109
  exiting, WIN 17
  installing, WIN 31–33
  navigating within, WIN 12–14
  pinning, WIN 110–112
  running from Apps list, WIN 110
  running using Search box, WIN 23–25
  running using Start screen, WIN 11–12
  switching between, WIN 16–17, WIN 27
  unpinning, WIN 113–114
APP bar, **WIN 11**

B

background pattern, Start screen, changing, WIN 103

C

charms, WIN 15–16
  returning to Start screen, WIN 15–16
  searching apps, WIN 28–29
  searching the Internet, WIN 25–27
  sharing using, WIN 30
clearing Search box, WIN 61
clicking, WIN 6
Clipboard, **WIN 67**
closing Local Disk (C:) dialog box, WIN 54
cloud computing, WIN 94
color scheme, Start screen, changing, WIN 102–103

computer
  shutting down, WIN 39–40
  turning off, WIN 80
computer viruses. *See* viruses
copy and paste method, **WIN 67**
copying, **WIN 67**
  files to Pictures library, WIN 67–69
copyrights, **WIN 65**, WIN 65–66
customizing Windows 8, using a Microsoft account, WIN 4

D

definitions, **APP 21**
deleting folders from Pictures library, WIN 80
details pane
  displaying folder properties, WIN 57
  displaying Local Disk (C:) properties, WIN 52–53
disk(s), hard, WIN 51
disk labels, **WIN 51**
displaying
  Action Center, APP 9–12
  apps, WIN 109
  folder properties in details pane, WIN 57
  folder properties in Properties dialog box, WIN 58
  Local Disk (C:) dialog box, WIN 53–54
  Local Disk (C:) properties in details pane, WIN 52–53
  Windows desktop, WIN 17–18
double-clicking, WIN 6
double-taps, WIN 4
dragging, WIN 5, WIN 6
drives, viewing contents, WIN 56

E

exiting apps, WIN 17

F

file(s)
  copying to Pictures library, WIN 67–69
  hidden, WIN 59
  multiple, moving into folders, WIN 71

  searching for, WIN 59–61
  zipped, **WIN 78**, WIN 78–80
File Explorer, WIN 19
folder windows, **WIN 50,** WIN 50–59
  details pane, WIN 52–53, WIN 57
  displaying Windows folder properties, WIN 57–58
  Local Disk (C:) drive Properties dialog box, WIN 53–54
  maximizing, WIN 51
  opening, WIN 51
  previewing folder properties, WIN 57
  switching folders using address bar, WIN 55–56
  viewing contents of drives, WIN 56
  viewing folder contents, WIN 59
folders
  creating in Pictures library, WIN 69–70
  deleting from Pictures library, WIN 80
  displaying properties in details pane, WIN 57
  displaying properties in Properties dialog box, WIN 58
  hidden, WIN 59
  moving multiple files into, WIN 71
  previewing properties, WIN 57
  refreshing images on, WIN 72
  searching for, WIN 59–61
  viewing contents, WIN 59
  zipping, WIN 78
free-spinning the mouse wheel, WIN 6

G

gestures, **WIN 4**, WIN 5

H

hackers, **APP 9**
hard disks, **WIN 51**
hidden files and folders, WIN 59

I

images, refreshing on folders, WIN 72
installing

IND 1

apps, WIN 31–33
updates, automatically, APP 19–20
Internet, **WIN 2**
    searching using charms,
        WIN 25–27
intranets, **WIN 2**
item check boxes, WIN 66

K

keyboard(s)
    layouts, WIN 7
    on-screen, WIN 5
keyboard shortcuts, **WIN 7**

L

layouts, keyboards, WIN 7
live tiles, **WIN 10**
    turning off, WIN 114–115
local accounts, **WIN 91**
    adding to user accounts,
        WIN 94–98
Local Disk (C:) dialog box
    closing, WIN 54
    displaying, WIN 53–54
lock screen, **WIN 8**
    personalizing, WIN 100–102

M

malware, **APP 9**
    protecting against, APP 21–24
maximizing windows
    folder windows, WIN 51
    Snap, WIN 63
Microsoft accounts, **APP 1,**
    WIN 91–93
    adding to user accounts,
        WIN 98–99
    creating, APP 1–7, WIN 92–93
    customizing Windows 8, WIN 4
    signing in, WIN 99
minimizing windows
    Shake, WIN 62
    Show Desktop button,
        WIN 63–64
mouse, WIN 6
mouse wheel operations, WIN 6
moving
    multiple files into folders,
        WIN 71
    tiles, WIN 20
    tiles between tile groups, WIN 118

N

naming tile groups, WIN 119–122
navigating within an app,
    WIN 12–14
notification area, **WIN 18**

O

on-screen keyboards, WIN 5
opening
    folder windows, WIN 51
    windows, WIN 61
    Windows Firewall window,
        APP 14
operating systems, **WIN 2**

P

passwords, **WIN 7**
    picture. *See* picture passwords
pasting, **WIN 67**
Photos app, **WIN 65, WIN 75**
    viewing pictures, WIN 75–76
picture passwords, **WIN 7,**
    WIN 104, WIN 104–108
    creating, WIN 104–108
    security, WIN 108
Pictures library, WIN 65–77
    copying files to, WIN 67–69
    creating folders in, WIN 69–70
    deleting folders, WIN 80
    moving multiple files into,
        WIN 71
    refreshing images, WIN 72
    searching for pictures,
        WIN 66
    viewing and changing properties
        of pictures, WIN 72–75
    viewing images, WIN 75–76
    viewing pictures as slide show,
        WIN 76–77
pinching, WIN 5
pinning apps, WIN 110–112
pointing, WIN 6
pressing
    mouse wheel, WIN 6
    thumb button, WIN 6
pressing and holding, WIN 4
previewing folder properties,
    WIN 57
properties, **WIN 52**
    folders, previewing, WIN 57
    folders, displaying in details pane,
        WIN 57

folders, displaying in Properties
    dialog box, WIN 58
Local Disk (C:), displaying,
    WIN 52–53
Local Disk (C:) dialog box,
    WIN 53–54
pictures, viewing anc changing,
    WIN 72–75
Properties dialog box, displaying
    folder properties, WIN 58

R

Recycle Bin, **WIN 18**
reordering tile groups, WIN 118–119
resizing tiles, WIN 21–22
Restart command, **WIN 8**
restoring windows, WIN 64–75
    Shake, WIN 62
right-clicking, WIN 6
right-dragging, WIN 6
rotating the mouse wheel,
    WIN 6
running apps from Apps list,
    WIN 110

S

ScreenTips, **WIN 57**
scroll arrows, **WIN 6,** WIN 7
scroll bar, **WIN 6,** WIN 7
scroll boxes, **WIN 6,** WIN 7
scrolling, WIN 6
Search box, **WIN 59**
    running apps using, WIN 23–25
searching
    apps, using charms, WIN 28–29
    for files and folders, WIN 59–61
    Internet, using charms,
        WIN 25–27
security, APP 9–24
    picture passwords, WIN 108
    Windows Defender. *See* Windows
        Defender
    Windows Firewall. *See* Windows
        Firewall
    Windows Update, **APP 19,**
        APP 19–20
Semantic Zoom, **WIN 108,**
    WIN 108–109
servers, **WIN 2**
Shake, WIN 62
sharing, using charms, WIN 30

Show Desktop button, minimizing windows, WIN 63–64
Shut down command, **WIN 8**
shutting down
  computers, WIN 39–40
  options, WIN 8
  Windows 8, WIN 37–40
sign-in screen, WIN 8
signing in to an account, WIN 8–10
  Microsoft accounts, WIN 99
signing out of an account, WIN 37–38
SkyDrive, **WIN 91**
Sleep command, **WIN 8**
slide shows, **WIN 76**, WIN 76–77
  ending, WIN 77
  viewing, WIN 76–77
Snap, maximizing windows, WIN 63
spyware, **APP 9**
Start screen, **WIN 2, WIN 10**
  changing background pattern, WIN 103
  changing color scheme, WIN 102–103
  customizing, WIN 108–115
  displaying all apps, WIN 109
  pinning apps, WIN 110–112
  returning to, WIN 15–16, WIN 19
  running apps, WIN 11–12
  running apps from Apps list, WIN 110
  turning off live tiles, WIN 114–115
  unpinning apps, WIN 113–114
starting
  Windows 8, WIN 7–10
  Windows Help and Support, WIN 33–36
stretching, WIN 5
strong passwords, WIN 7
swiping, WIN 5
switching
  between apps, WIN 16–17, WIN 27
  folders, address bar, WIN 55–56

T

taps, WIN 4
taskbar, **WIN 18**

thumb button, pressing, WIN 6
tile(s)
  moving, WIN 20
  resizing, WIN 21–22
tile groups, **WIN 108**
  creating, WIN 117
  moving tiles between, WIN 118
  naming, WIN 119–122
  reordering, WIN 118–119
  viewing, WIN 115–116
tile layout, WIN 115–122
tilting the mouse wheel, WIN 6
touch screens, WIN 4–5
triple-clicking, WIN 6

U

unpinning apps, WIN 113–114
user accounts, **WIN 7, WIN 90,** WIN 90–91
  adding local accounts, WIN 94–98
  adding Microsoft accounts, WIN 98–99
  setting up, WIN 94–99
  signing in to, WIN 8–10
  signing out of, WIN 37–38
user icons, **WIN 7**
user names, **WIN 7**

V

viewing
  drive contents, WIN 56
  folder contents, WIN 59
  pictures in Photos app, WIN 75–76
  properties of pictures, WIN 72–75
  slide shows, WIN 76–77
  tile groups, WIN 115–116
  zipped folder contents, WIN 79
viruses, **APP 9**
  definitions, APP 21
  protecting against, APP 21–24

W

windows
  folder. *See* folder windows
  maximizing using Snap, WIN 63
  minimizing using Show Desktop button, WIN 63–64

  opening, WIN 61
  restoring, WIN 64–75
  Shake to minimize and restore, WIN 62
Windows 8, **WIN 2**
  customizing using a Microsoft account, WIN 4
  shutting down, WIN 37–40
  starting, WIN 7–10
  system requirements, WIN 3
Windows 8 Enterprise, **WIN 3**
Windows 8 Pro, **WIN 3**
Windows 8 RT, **WIN 3**
Windows Defender, APP 13, **APP 13**, APP 21–24
  scanning using, APP 21–23
  viewing settings for automatic scanning, APP 24
Windows desktop, WIN 18
  displaying, WIN 17–18
Windows Firewall, **APP 13,** APP 13–18
  allowing features through, APP 14–16
  disallowing features through, APP 17–18
  opening Windows Firewall window, APP 14
Windows folder, searching for files and folders, WIN 60
Windows Help and Support, **WIN 33,** WIN 33–37
  browsing Help, WIN 33–36
  starting, WIN 33–36
Windows SmartScreen, **APP 13**
Windows Update, **APP 19,** APP 19–20
  installing updates automatically, APP 19–20
workstations, **WIN 2**
worms, **APP 9**
wrist injury, minimizing, WIN 6

Z

zipped files, **WIN 78,** WIN 78–89
zooming, viewing tile groups, WIN 115–116